CLUBSMARTS

CLUBS

Buying Golf Clubs that Work

Jonathan Abrahams

• • • • • •

LYONS & BURFORD, PUBLISHERS

Printed in the United States of America

Design by MRP
Illustrations by Manuel F. Cheo

10 9 8 7 6 5 4 3 2 1

Library of Congress Cataloging-in-Publication Data

Abrahams, Jonathan.
Clubsmarts: choosing clubs that work / Jonathan Abrahams.
p. cm.
ISBN 1-55821-272-8
1. Golf clubs (Sporting goods) I. Title. II. Title: Clubsmarts
GV976.A27 1994
796.352′082—dc20 93-43262
CIP

Contents

Acknowledgments

The Author would like to thank the following people for their generous assistance: James A. Frank and Rob Sauerhaft of GOLF *Magazine,* Pete Piotrowski of Aldila, Inc., Bill Moretti, PGA, of The Academy of Golf Dynamics, and Tom Galvin of the PGA of America.

Foreword

The first game I learned as a kid was baseball. "I wanna baseball mitt," I announced, and my father dutifully drove me down to the local sporting goods store, where they had a big selection. Dad grabbed the smallest glove he could find, and told me to slip my hand in it. I did. "How does that feel?" he asked. I looked at the name autographed in the palm. It said Willie Mays. "Fine," I said. Sold.

Later that day my father threw a few balls to me. I caught some; I dropped some. I didn't hold Willie responsible for any of it. Baseball is such a nice, simple game. Throw, catch, hit. Maybe that's why it was our national pastime.

Today, however, it could be argued that golf is our national pastime. It's not official, but look at the evidence: more golf courses being built, more people taking golf vacations, greater attendance at golf schools and camps, in the cities, in the suburbs, *there are just more people playing the game.* The stigma of golf being a game for the idle rich is gone.

The thing is, golf is not a simple game. You can't just walk into your local sporting goods store, find an autograph you like, and walk out with your new set of clubs. Hit a few bad shots and it may be perfectly legitimate to blame it on the clubs. Why? Because if your clubs don't fit, you'll be forced to compensate by unnaturally altering your swing. It's like a pair of shoes; if they don't fit, they'll probably make you walk funny.

Take the case of John Daly, the PGA Tour's Golfer For the Common Man, 1991 PGA Champion, and possessor of the longest and most powerful swing on Tour. He makes numerous mistakes during the swing, but compensates for them with tremendous natural talent and athletic ability. Often he is spectacular, but occasionally he is awful, knocking the ball all over the course. One could only blame this inconsistency on a long, loose swing that dips the club well past parallel at the top and is difficult to control.

I had the opportunity to spend three days with John filming an instructional video a few months after his victory in the PGA Championship. I asked him where that long swing of his came from. "I've had it since I was a kid," he told me. "My dad gave me a set of Jack Nicklaus autograph clubs when I was real small. They were so heavy that when I took the club back, it just fell over my back. I've swung the same ever since."

Aha. Blame Jack. Of course, things worked out okay for John despite everything, but chances are with his talent, he would be a great golfer no matter what. His ability doesn't depend on his extra-long swing; in fact, one might say his ability survives in spite of it. Had he started with clubs that actually fit, his swing would be shorter and more consistent. And strong as he is, he wouldn't lose much distance. John's going to hit it long even if he only takes the club halfway back.

The point is, you, me, and just about every other golfer on the planet who isn't John Daly doesn't have the ability to compensate for poorly fit equipment and still play well. Golf is too precise a game. Think about this: If your 5-iron is a half-inch too long for you, the club will sit about a quarter-inch too far toward the heel. This closes the clubface about 2 degrees. Make a perfect swing and your ball doesn't hit the green; it finds the left bunker. This happens a couple of times and you start compensating; to fight the hook, you make a strong lateral move with your body toward the target. It works a few times, but then your body gets so far out ahead of the ball that you're either pushing the ball well to the right or hitting snap-hooks. What a mess—and all because of an extra half-inch. If the clubs had fit, this never would have happened.

Yet most golfers, good, bad, or somewhere in the middle, are unaware of the relationship between clubs that fit and a good golf game. They know very little about equipment except what they see on television commercials and what appeals to them when they look around in the shop. Armed with this ignorance, they shell out hundreds, sometimes thousands of dollars on new clubs, believing that their investment is going to help them play better. You can spend a million dollars; if your clubs don't fit, you're not going to play good golf. If only everybody knew that, they'd all play better and enjoy the game more.

That's why, I think, *Clubsmarts* is a book that needed to be written. Digest all the information in these pages and you'll not only know golf equipment but the ins and outs of the actual process of buying it. You'll have a tremendous advantage over the uneducated shopper. While they'll be basically taking shots in the dark to find the right set of clubs, you'll go confidently through the clubfitting process. The result will be equipment that allows you to improve at the fastest rate possible. You may not hit every shot perfectly, but at least you'll know you can't blame Willie when you miss. Or whomever.

—JONATHAN ABRAHAMS
New York, New York
February, 1994

ONE

The Golf Club

Golf is very much a scientific game, and any discussion of the equipment that is used to play it involves technical, golf-specific terminology. Before you speed out to the nearest pro shop, wallet in hand, it's a good idea to make sure you're well versed in the lingo of golf club construction.

Let's talk generalities first. Every golf club is different, but all possess a number of universal characteristics. These are the basic properties of the golf club.

Clubhead

The clubhead is the implement. It is what ultimately makes contact with the golf ball and sends it on its way. Clubheads may be made of a number of things, but, regardless of material, are described as either woods or irons. Wood heads are larger, pear-shaped implements, whereas irons are smaller, blade-like tools.

Clubface

The clubface is the hitting area of the clubhead. It is flat or nearly flat, and usually scored with vertical grooves, horizontal grooves, or both. All clubfaces, with the exception of some putters, have loft. Loft means the clubface is angled upward, from as little as seven to nearly 65 degrees. Loft is what produces an airborne shot, and the rule of thumb is that the less loft, the longer the shot will fly if struck well. Clubs are assigned numbers according to how much loft the clubface has. For example, a 1-wood (driver) may have 11 degrees of loft, a 3-wood 15 degrees, and a 5-wood 20 degrees. The higher the number, the more loft and the shorter the shot produced.

All clubheads have a very important characteristic called lie. Lie refers to the angle formed by the centerline of the shaft and the ground, when the clubhead is properly soled with the clubface perpendicular, or square to the target. If the club does not sit flat on the ground, the clubface cannot be square to the target, and errant shots result.

Grooves

Scored in the clubface, grooves can run horizontally and vertically. Vertical grooves are generally alignment aids; they either frame the hitting area or sweet spot and provide a reference parallel, or running with, the target.

Horizontal grooves are more interesting, and the subject of some debate. Popular belief says that horizontal grooves help "grab" the golf ball at impact, and therefore, create backspin. (Backspin allows a ball to rise in the air and stop quickly upon landing, a must for accurate shots.) If the grooves are too deep, say golf's governing bodies, too much backspin will be created, giving the golfer an unfair advantage. For that reason, the overseers of the rules of golf in the United States and Europe, the United States Golf Association and the Royal & Ancient Golf Club, have established limits on equipment manufacturers as to the size and shape of horizontal grooves.

For the consumer, however, the grooves debate is virtually superfluous: Because of the USGA and R&A's regulations, there is not a wide variety of groove sizes available. Grooves are almost identical from manufacturer to manufacturer.

Shaft

Of all the components that go into the construction of a golf club, the shaft is the most important variable. True, the clubhead actually hits the ball, but without the shaft, the clubhead wouldn't swing. In many ways, the properties of a certain shaft determine how the club will be swung.

Most important is the flex of the shaft (the measurement of its resistance to bending under a given stress). The general rule is that, if all other variables are constant, a more flexible shaft will send the ball higher into the air than a stiff shaft. However, as you will discover later in this book, there are too many variables in golf club manufacturing to make this rule etched in stone.

The Rules of Golf state that the shaft must be of a circular shape and extend straight from the clubhead to the end of the grip, but other than that, there are no restrictions. There is a standard length for most men's clubs—a driver, the longest club in the bag, is generally 43 inches long, with shorter clubs descending in half-inch increments—but you can order any length of club you wish. Therefore, shafts are available in many different sizes, weights, materials, and, consequently, with many different properties. Steel, graphite, titanium, and mixtures of the three are just some of the materials available. Each of these materials and combinations of materials have distinct characteristics as to size, weight, and performance. One of the biggest challenges facing he consumer today is finding the shaft that best suits the individual's game.

Grip

This sleeve of rubber or leather at the end of the shaft may seem relatively insignificant, but there's no denying its importance: It is the only connection between your hands and the club. Although there has been comparatively little technological advancement in grip construction (grips have been, on the whole, made of rubber or leather for decades), there is a wide variety of grips on the market. Your concern should be finding one that you find comfortable to put your hands on and swing the club with.

Putting It All Together

Add the components, and presto, you've got a golf club. Knowing the basic parts of a club, however, is not enough. There are different categories of clubs—woods, irons, wedges, putters—as well as sub-

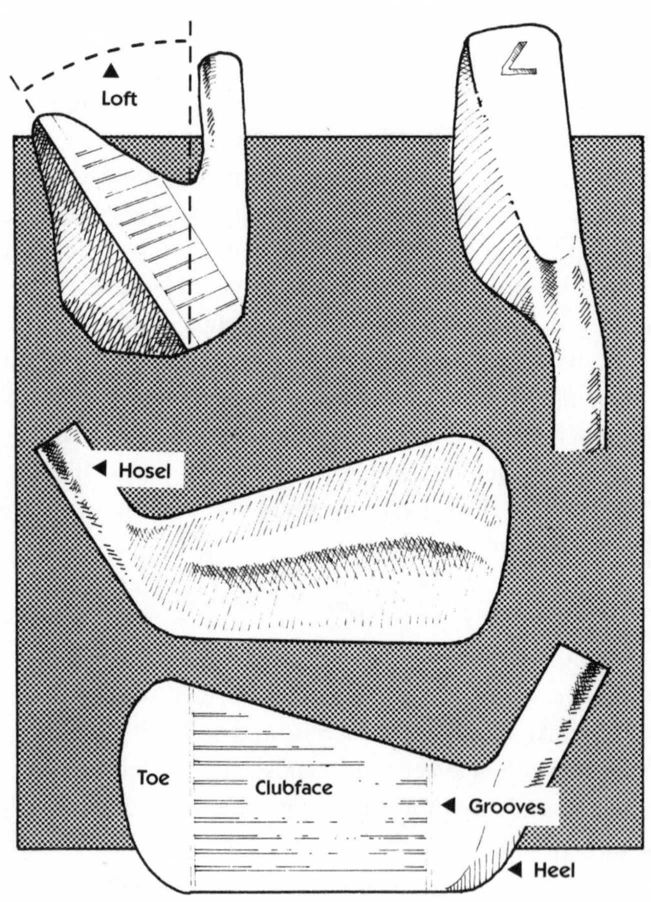

Iron head

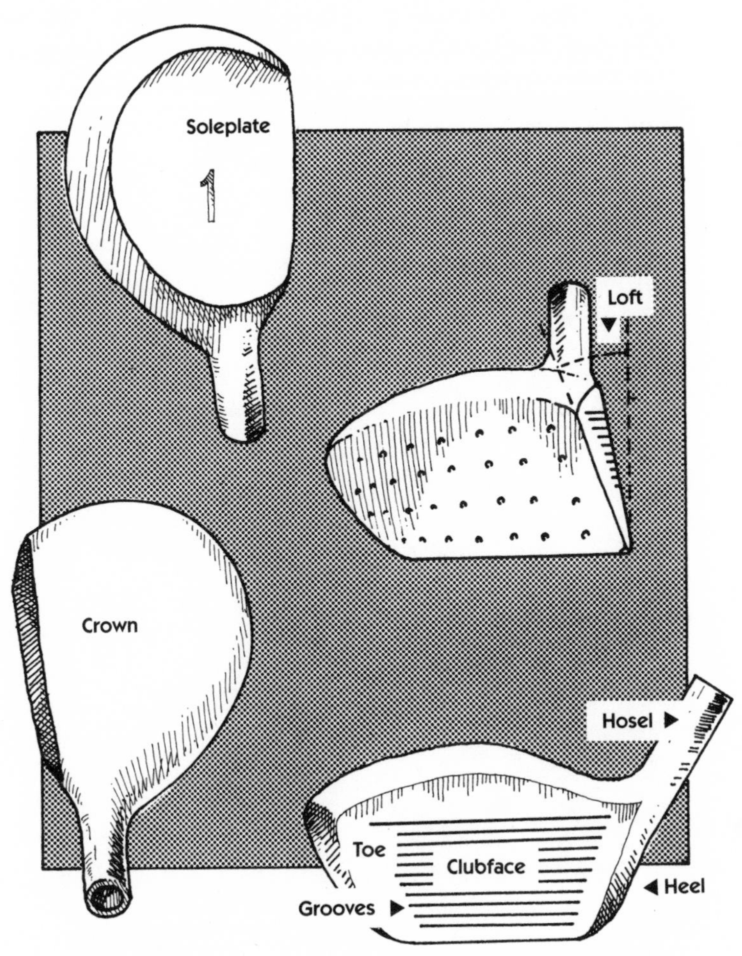

Wood head

categories within these categories. To make a truly intelligent choice, you must have very specific knowledge of what equipment is available, which means exploring each of the categories and their subcategories fully. That's coming up.

The average amateur is less equipment-knowledgeable than this very short first chapter. He or she relies on short magazine articles or even advertisements for information. So you're already ahead of the game—but the learning has barely just begun.

TWO

Know Yourself

You may walk into an equipment-packed golf shop for the first time with a feeling of helplessness. "Look at all this stuff," you might say. "It all looks the same." Yet the experienced golf consumer is, if anything, impressed by the selection. "So many clubs," he or she says, "and each one of them different."

Funny thing is, you're both right. It's true: At first glance, most golf clubs *do* look the same. As we said in Chapter 1, they all have a clubhead, shaft, and grip, and they're all used the same way. Whack the ball out into the wild blue yonder, right?

Well, okay, kind of, but there's another side to the story. Golf club manufacturing is such a precise business that the smallest tweaking can completely change the characteristics of the basic form. Good players prefer head shape X; high handicappers gravitate toward head shape Y. Shaft W performs better in the wind than shaft Z but provides less feel for those with weaker hands. Feature Q fights the dreaded slice; R guards against the occasional hook. Manufacturers, eager to impress, want to personalize their clubs to each individual golfer as much as possible, so options are as vast as promises of a better game are frequent. It's enough to make you *golf loony.*

Don't go bouncing off the walls yet, however. You can eliminate some, but not all, of the confusion by knowing your game. Identify your strengths, weaknesses, shot patterns, and tendencies. Once you truly know your game, it's like blood typing: You'll find that a big chunk of the equipment out there simply doesn't mix with your kind of golf, and you can eliminate it from consideration.

So, before we go through the haystack of golf clubs, let's make sure you have a good idea of *you the golfer.* Do you hit the ball long and wild? Straight and short? Do you slice the ball? Have problems getting it airborne? You need to be sure before going any further because references will be made to different types of golfers as the book progresses. It'll make finding that shiny little needle much easier.

Evaluate your game by answering all of the following questions. Don't think in terms of where your game should be or what you are capable of doing on the course. Think in terms of the truth—what you actually accomplish each time you play. Be honest—first of all, nobody's going to see the answers but you, and if you let your ego get in the way chances are you'll ultimately wind up with equipment that doesn't suit your game.

1. How many times a year do you play? 0–10 10–25 25–50 50+
2. Average score: under 80 80–90 90–100 100+
3. How far do you hit a driver, on average? ______ yds
4. What club would you use for a 150-yard shot? ______
5. How many times per round does your drive find the fairway, on average? 0–4 4–7 7–11 11+
6. How many greens do you hit per round in regulation, on average? 0–4 4–8 8–12 12+
7. What is the usual shape of your shots? (*See illustration*) straight right-to-right right-to-left left-to-right left-to-left
8. What is the usual trajectory of your shots? low medium high
9. Do you take a divot with: short irons mid-irons long irons fairway woods driver?

Simply answering these questions is helpful. It forces you to look at your game honestly, and come to conclusions about your strengths and weaknesses. It should also give you an idea of what type of golfer you are. Now, of course, no two people are exactly alike, but you

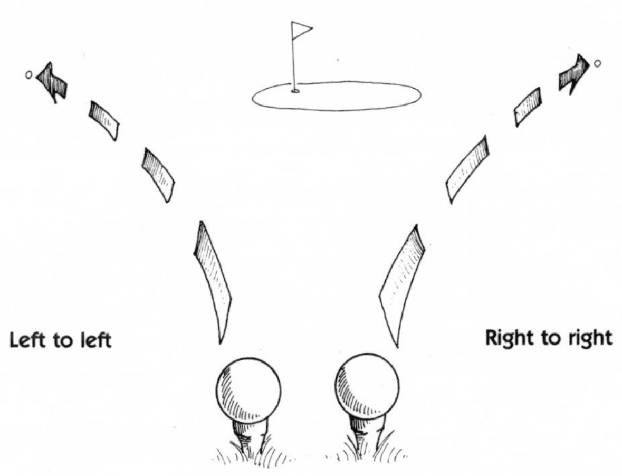

Shot trajectories

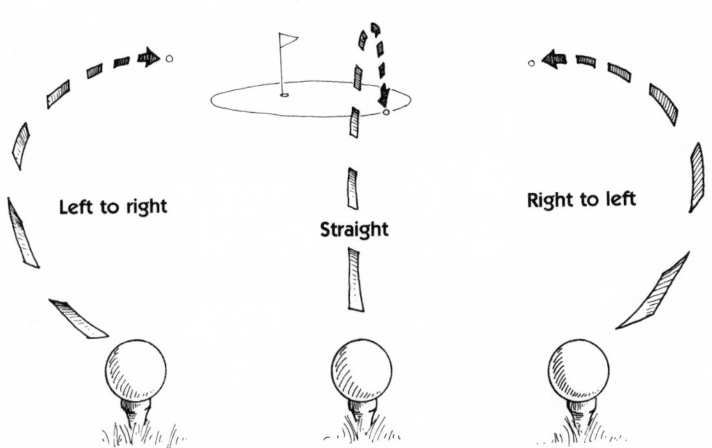

should be able to find yourself and your golf game in one of the following five categories.

Thirtysomething

You can be any age to be a Thirtysomething. It refers to your handicap, which is somewhere between thirty and . . . well, it's *up* there. You don't play or practice that often, and when you do, your score is somewhere around 110. Hitting fairways and greens isn't an issue; getting the ball airborne is your prime objective. You'd like to break 100 regularly and avoid the annoying topped shots and whiffs that find their way into your rounds. You need a set of clubs that you can learn and improve with.

Bananaballer

Many golfers slice the ball. For you, however, the slice defines your game. Every shot, no matter where it starts, bends to the right. This costs you distance you can't aford to lose. The idea of hitting a straight shot, not to mention right-to-left, is completely foreign to you. You take a divot with every club in the back except perhaps the driver, and the divots are deep. You hit a few fairways and an occasional green, but you spend a lot of time in the right rough. Breaking 90 would make you very happy. Your golf clubs should help reduce the effects ofyour slice, yet still be playable when and if you finally straighten it out.

Bunter

Your partners tell you stories about what the rough is like, but you've never seen it for yourself. You just bunt every shot straight down the middle. Your problem is a lack of distance. It takes you three shots to reach greens that your buddies reach in two. Odds are you hit 10 or more fairways a round, but only a few greens, because they're just a few yards out of your reach. You'd also like to hit it a little higher. If you're smart, you've compensated for your lack of length by developing a deft short game. This could keep your handicap near single digits. If not, 90-plus scores could be routine. You need a set of clubs that will produce no less than your maximum potential for distance without sacrificing your strength, accuracy.

Bomber

Hit it long: That's your game. The longer the shot the better, so you live for the tee shot. You swing hard enough that your shot patterns are inconsistent: sometimes left, sometimes right. Chances are you hit more greens than fairways, because your strength and length enables you to recover from the rough. Combine wildness with your distance and you get spectacular, roller-coaster rounds: a few birdies, a few too many double bogeys. Get a set of clubs that will help you straighten it out and you could be in the 70s.

Player

As they say in the South, you can flat play. And you do—a lot. Golf is something you do more than once a week during the season, and consequently you have a fine-tuned swing that's pretty reliable. You count on breaking eighty each time you tee it up. For you, the right set of clubs means comfort and playability. With comfort comes confidence, and with playability comes the knowledge of what you can and cannot do with each golf shot. You don't want any surprises with your golf clubs.

None of these characters may describe you and your golf game perfectly, but one should come pretty close. Keep your new alter ego in mind, because we will be speaking in terms of these five golfers throughout the book.

THREE

What's Available

As we've said, options are plentiful to a fault in the world of golf equipment, so there is going to be a good deal of information for you to digest. However, having a strong sense of your playing characteristics should help you to sift out the information that is pertinent to your game. We'll break it up into three basic parts: clubhead, shaft, and grip. Sounds simple, right? Wait until it gets specific.

Clubhead

There are several different basic clubhead designs for both woods and irons. What's most important is knowing the characteristics of each and being able to identify them when you walk into your local golf shop.

Irons

Generally, the most important feature in the construction of an iron clubhead is the distribution of weight. Weight is often the determining factor when clubmakers set out to design a club. An iron designed for a tour player's iron, for example, usually has the weight distributed differently from one made for your average Thirtysomething.

There are three basic iron clubhead designs, each with a different distribution of weight.

Traditional blades—the choice of most professionals, these clubheads are, indeed, for The Player only. With the majority of the weight

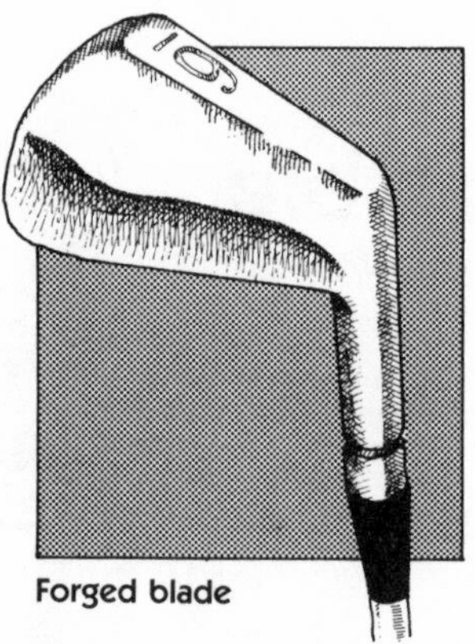

Forged blade

centered behind the optimal hitting area on the clubface, or sweet spot, traditional blades do not offer much margin for error. Mis-hit a shot and not only will you get much less distance, but the shock of poor contact will send a vibration through your fingertips that sometimes feels like it affects the entire body.

If, however, you are at that level that just about every shot you hit is on the sweet spot, then blades may be for you. Most blades are made from cold forged steel, a process in which heat-softened steel is pounded into a basic shape, then hardened under extreme cold before it is ground and polished into a finished product. This produces a clubhead that feels "soft" when solid contact is made—a feature that the better player likes because it allows him to maneuver the ball up, down, left or right easily. Dependability is also a selling point. "No surprises," is what you'll hear low handicappers say. "What you see is what you get." It's true: You'll never have to worry about the ball exploding off the clubface and producing a mysterious ten extra yards. There's also aesthetic appeal: Low handicappers appreciate the clean, simple look of a traditional blade, sometimes described as "classic."

Perimeter-weighted—also known as cavity-backed or heel-toe weighted—clubs are far more common than traditional blades, accounting for better than 3/4 of the iron market. Most perimeter-weighted clubs are

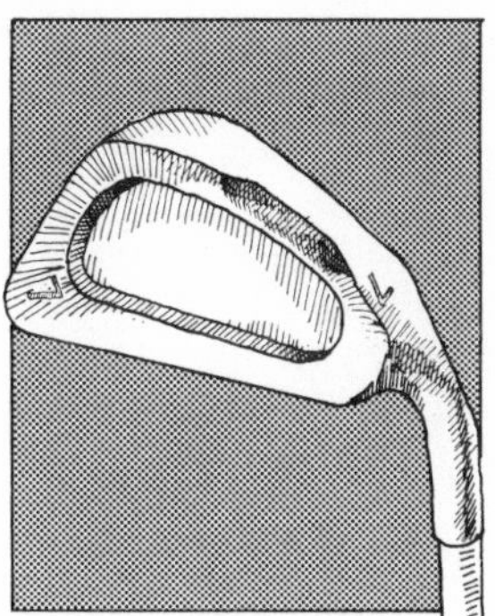

Perimeter-weighted iron

made from the casting process, which involves making a mold from a wax model, then mass producing clubheads by pouring molten steel, or occasionally graphite, into the mold. Clubmakers opt for casting because it's cheaper, more efficient, and allows for a wider variety of head designs than the hand-pounded process of cold forging.

The real reason perimeter-weighted clubs are so popular is that they are, generally, just plain easier to hit than traditional blades. With the weight around the perimeter, the sweet spot is larger, allowing more margin for error. They're more forgiving, too: Mis-hit a shot and the results won't be quite as bad. Good players sometimes shy away from these clubs because the casting process produces a head with a slightly harder feel and less playability. These golfers, however, are few and far between. Simply put, unless you're threatening par every time you play, you should be playing perimeter-weighted clubs.

The casting process enables manufacturers to be very precise about where the weight should be deposited in a clubhead. Research proved that all the weight doesn't have to be centered directly behind the sweet spot for a good shot to come off. The key, the manufacturers discovered, is ensuring that the weight is balanced around the sweet spot. So, as the name suggests, weight was removed from the center of the clubhead and redistributed around the perimeter, where mis-hits occur. Hit a perimeter-weighted club off the toe, for example, and the redistributed weight helps compensate for the mis-hit, so there is less vibration, and more important, less drop-off in distance.

That's the basic concept of perimeter-weighting, but there are, of course, variations. Every manufacturer has a slightly different distribution of weight in its clubhead, so it's important that you know what the different designs will do for you.

Many perimeter-weighted clubs will have a high concentration of weight toward the sole of the club. When contact is made, the majority of the clubhead's weight is under the equator of the ball, which helps get it airborne. Thirtysomethings who have trouble getting the ball in the air or Bunters in search of a higher trajectory should look for a good deal of *sole-weighting* in their irons.

Other manufacturers distribute the majority of the weight in the heel and toe of the clubhead, bookending the sweet spot. The theory is that amateurs mis-hit most of their shots in the heel or toe, so when they do, the weight is there to compensate and they lose less distance. If you have trouble finding the sweet spot, look for clubs with generous *heel-toe weighting.*

A recent trend among clubmakers is to remove weight from the neck, or hosel of the clubhead, and redistribute it in the hitting area. This allows the manufacturer to add more weight to the "trouble spots" (heel, toe, sole) without increasing the overall weight of the clubhead.

Forged Cavity Back—In an effort to combine the best of both worlds, manufacturers have recently developed cavity-backed clubs made from the forging process. There isn't as much perimeter weighting as casting allows, so the clubs aren't quite as easy to hit or forgiving. Wild Bananaballers or Thirtysomethings may not be ready for these clubs. However, for the better or rapidly improving golfer, forged cavity backs offer a nice combination of feel and forgiveness.

Space Age—Some of the latest technology in the equipment industry has produced irons that aren't irons at all. That is to say, they're not made of metal. Graphite, Ceramic compound, and Melonite are finding their way into iron casting molds, resulting in new-age, new-look, high-cost clubs for those with heavy wallets. They're too

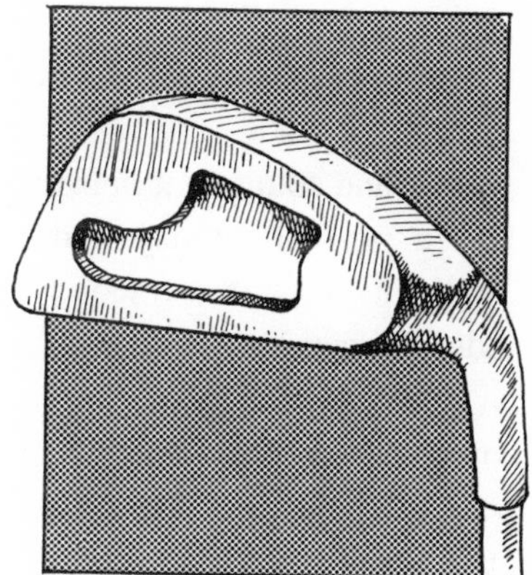

Heel-toe weighted iron

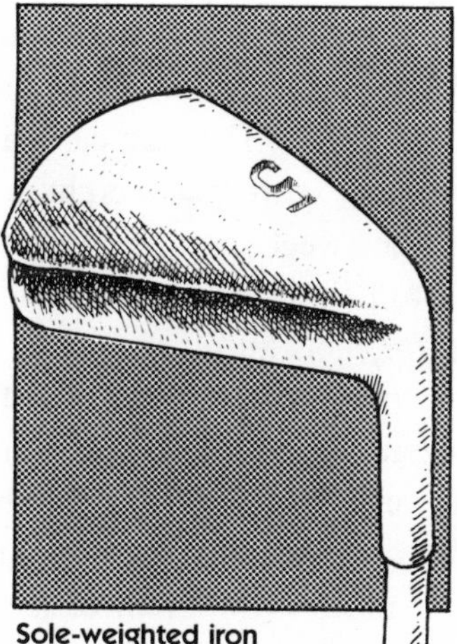

Sole-weighted iron

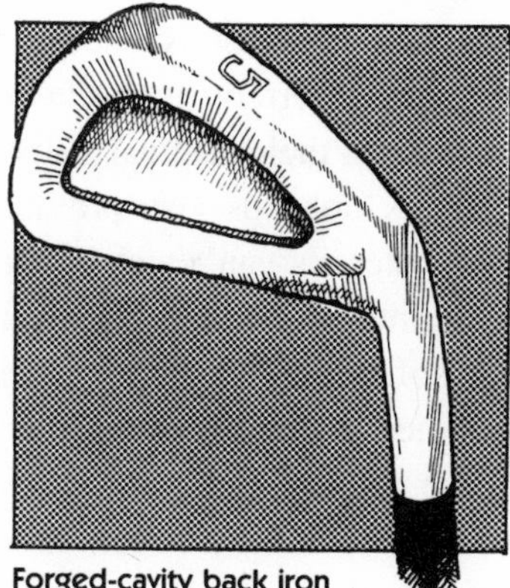

Forged-cavity back iron

new to make definitive statements about their playing properties, but generally, these clubs are designed for the mid-to-high handicapper.

Woods

There was a time when you could pick up a wood and count on it being made of actual wood. No more. Walk into a pro shop today and stainless steel woods, or "metal woods," will far outnumber "wood woods." You may even see more clubs made of graphite than wood. Still, it hasn't been phased out completely, and there are even rumblings in the industry of wood making a comeback.

Wood clubheads are carved out of blocks of either persimmon or laminated maple. They are carved into a rough shape, then the bottom is bored out, where lead weight is added. The majority of the weight is behind the sweet spot, meaning that a mis-hit shot doesn't have that weight to help it along. The result is a substantial drop-off in performance for shots hit off the sweet spot. For that reason, standard-sized wooden heads will do little for the golfer who fights inconsistency. Oversized heads are an exception, which you will read about later.

However, for the golfer who regularly finds the sweet spot, wooden clubs can provide great pleasure. There is nothing quite like looking down at the flowing grain of a persimmon driver in a mahogany or walnut stain. Persimmon woods are usually handmade with the sort of care that goes into fine cabinetry, and no two are exactly alike. For the player who truly has a *relationship* with his or her clubs, that is very appealing. In fact, many older persimmon woods made in the 40s, 50s, and 60s are so revered that they are referred to as "classics," and are bought by enthusiasts for many times their original value.

On a practical level, wooden clubheads also provide playability that, generally, woods of other materials can't match. Wood is softer than metal or graphite (bang it into something and you'll see) and therefore provides a bit of a softer feel at impact. Better players appreciate this because it gives them the feeling that they can "work" the ball—deliberately curving the ball to the left or right—because the ball stays on the clubface a split second longer. Persimmon is generally softer than laminated maple, and is therefore more popular.

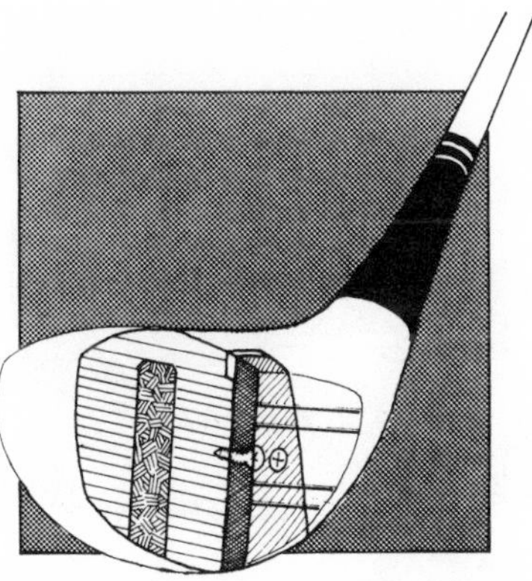

Persimmon wood. A solid block of wood, bored out, and filled with lead.

However, what every consumer should realize is that virtually every wooden clubhead has an insert in the sweet spot made of another material. Wood cannot withstand the pounding of impact over a long period of time without denting or chipping. The insert not only protects the clubface, but also plays a large part in determining the feel of the clubhead.

Most inserts are made of Cycolac, a high-impact plastic. It is a versatile material that withstands a great deal of abuse, while providing solid performance, characterized by a firm "click" at impact, yet enough "give" to allow a decent amount of playability. Other inserts are made of fiber, which is more expensive and less durable, but is softer, providing more "feel" and playability than Cycolac. Fiber can be found in most classic woodheads and today's top-of-the-line persimmon woods. Look in a Tour pro's bag: If he's got a persimmon wood, it's almost sure to have a fiber insert.

For everybody other than The Player, however, metalwoods are the most logical choice. Metalwoods began an equipment revolution in the late 1970s by embracing a simple concept of perimeter weighting designed, simply put, to make the game easier.

In contrast to the solid construction of wooden clubheads, **metal woods** are hollow, stainless steel shells filled with foam. The foam weighs next to nothing, meaning the weight of the clubhead can be

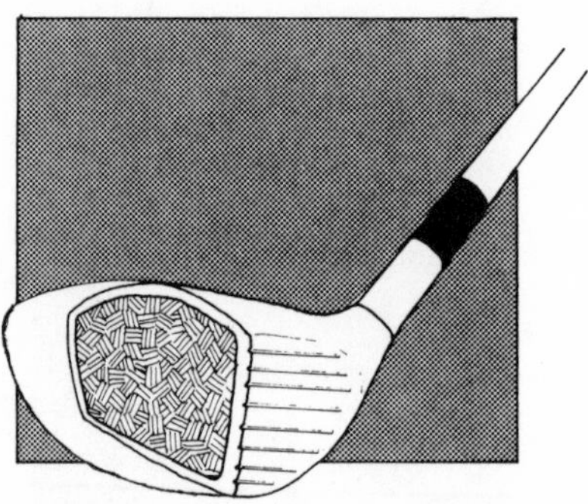

A metal wood head. A steel shell filled with foam produces a perimeter-weighted club.

distributed around the perimeter. The result is that mis-hits fly further and straighter because there's added weight in areas away from the sweet spot. Perimeter weighting also allows manufacturers to deposit a good portion of weight low in the clubhead, which will help the golfer get the ball airborne.

Additionally, steel is harder than Cycolac or fiber, meaning that the ball stays on the face a split second shorter at impact, resulting in less backspin. This produces more roll once the ball hits the fairway, which, for most amateurs, means more distance. Less backspin also means less sidespin, which translates into straighter shots, too. These are benefits the golf world has been quick to take advantage of: You'll find metal woods in nearly 75% of the golf bags in the United States.

Graphite woodheads are also making a dent in the club market. Graphite is lighter than steel, meaning that more weight can be distributed around the perimeter. It's also harder than wood, giving it many of the performance characteristics of metal. The result is a lightweight, forgiving, high performance club that, unfortunately, is much more expensive than metal or wood. Better players usually eschew graphite for metal or wood, but if you can afford it, try it out, no matter what your ability level. You may love the results.

Perimeter weighting has led to the latest development in equipment technology: **Oversized heads.** Advances in the manufacturing process

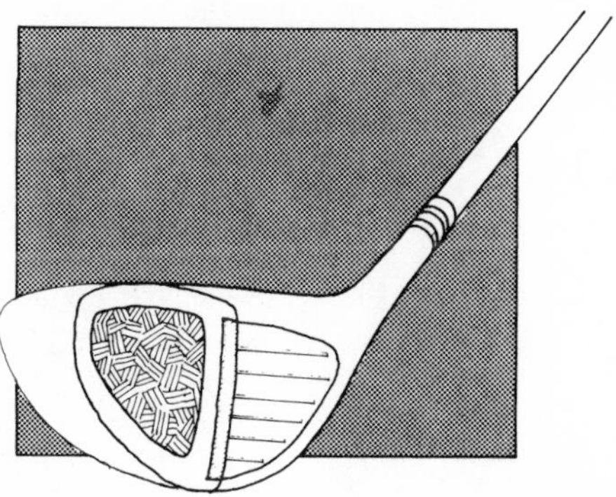

A graphite wood head. A graphite shell is filled with foam to form a strong, lightweight head.

of steel, as well as experiments with combinations of different metals, such as aluminum and titanium, has enabled companies to produce metals that are lighter and stronger. As a result, they are able to make larger heads without adding any weight. There are even a few oversized wood heads in production. It's too early to tell, but oversized heads may become the next revolution in manufacturing the same way metal woods did in the late 1970. By increasing the head size, manufacturers have enlarged the sweet spot, giving the amateur much more margin for error. For those that hit the ball squarely nearly every time, this doesn't mean much, but for everybody else (which accounts for more than 90% of all golfers) a larger sweet spot is a coup. Like the oversized tennis racquet, these "jumbos" have simply made the game easier. The benefits to Thirtysomethings, Bananaballers, and Bombers are obvious, but Players are embracing the larger heads as well. Others shy away, claiming the oversized heads allow them to get good results out of bad swings, great for the high handicapper, but breeding an unhealthy complacency for the better player.

There are interesting developments on the fringe of the industry. Clubs made of Kevlar, a space-age plastic used in bulletproof vests, have surfaced on the market, boasting the feel of wood and the performance of metal. Additionally, some metal woods can now be found with graphite inserts, which, manufacturers claim, remove

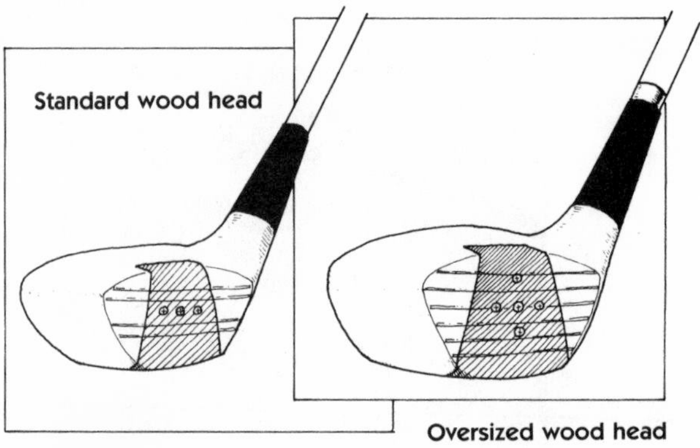

weight from the clubface. This allows them to redistribute the weight—you guessed it—around the perimeter.

Wedges

It's appropriate to give wedges their own category, because they are truly unique and personal clubs in a way that regular irons and woods are not. Most sets of irons include a **pitching wedge,** at 47–52 degrees the most lofted of the irons, and occasionally a **sand wedge,** which generally has between 53–59 degrees of loft and is designed for play out of the sand.

It's important to be discriminating about your wedges; there's no rule that says they must be the same make and model as the rest of your clubs. Not all sets include a sand wedge, and when they do, it is more than occasionally poorly designed. Yet a sand wedge is a vital part of your set makeup. You can try to play from the bunkers with a pitching wedge, but you won't be very successful; the club simply isn't designed to perform under such conditions. For that reason sand wedges are sold individually and assume the same sentimental value with the golfer as the putter and the driver.

What makes a sand wedge special is a property called "bounce," the angled flange attached to the bottom of the club. The bounce angle

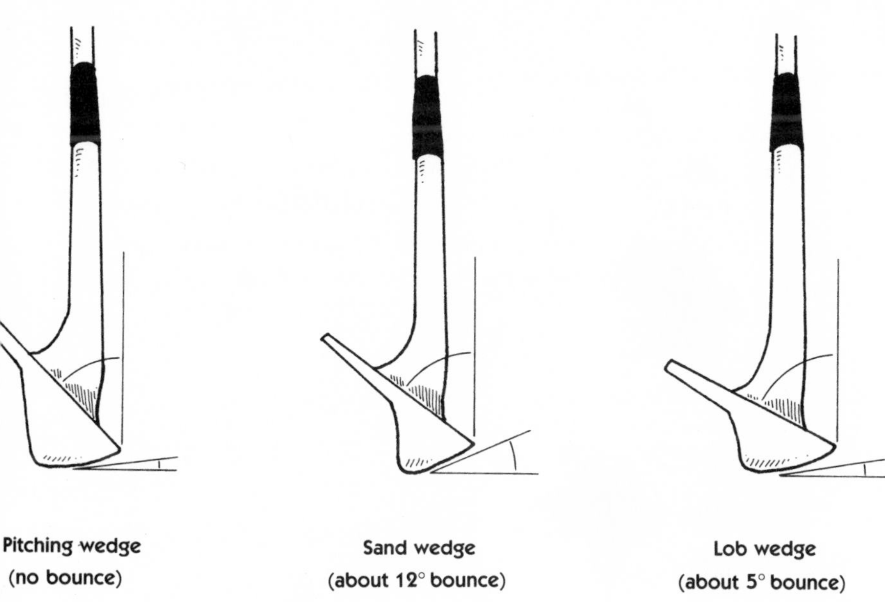

Pitching wedge (no bounce) | Sand wedge (about 12° bounce) | Lob wedge (about 5° bounce)

is the degree to which the trailing edge of the club is lower than the leading edge. A good sand wedge will have 10–13 degrees of bounce; this allows the club to slip through the sand easily. Bounce is also helpful when the club must make its way through heavy grass.

The more bounce, the higher the leading edge of the club when soled, so from tight lies in the fairway, sand wedges are not very effective. You can use a pitching wedge, which generally has about 5 degrees of bounce, but if your shot requires the added loft of a sand wedge, you need something else. Sort of a combination of the two, right?

Enter the third, or **lob wedge.** With more loft (60–65 degrees) than a sand wedge and bounce similar to a pitching wedge, the third wedge allows you to play high, short shots from the fairway. It's also useful for delicate shots around the green. Rarely will you find a set that includes a third wedge. Like sand wedges, they are sold individually.

Putters

Many people will argue that this is the most important club in the bag. The better you get, the more it's true; you can hit miserable full shots from tee-to-green all day long, but if you putt well, you'll still salvage a decent score when all is said and done. Putt poorly, however, and no matter how well you hit the ball, you won't score well.

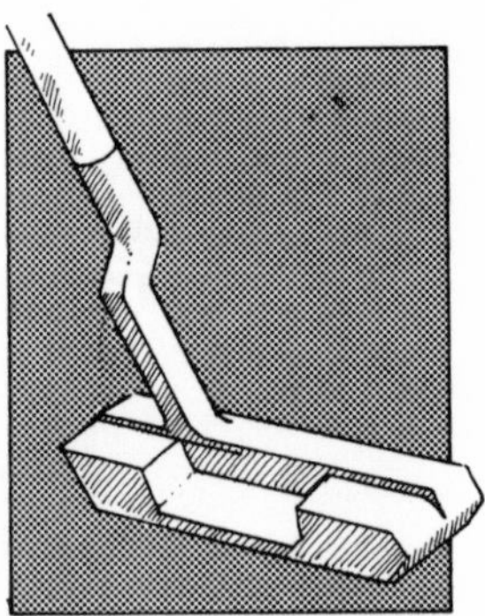

Heel-toe weighted putter

Blade putter

Flanged putter

Putters are available in countless sizes, shapes, and materials. Unlike other clubs, putters are universal; none are made with any one type of golfer in mind. It's a completely personal thing. Some have flat faces with no loft, some have slightly rounded faces with a few degrees of loft. There are offset hosels and straight hosels. You may find that straight-hoseled putters are a bit easier to align to the target than offset. Offset-hoseled putters, however, will often give a better feeling of rolling the ball, as opposed to hitting it, because the hands lead the clubhead in a bit of a dragging motion.

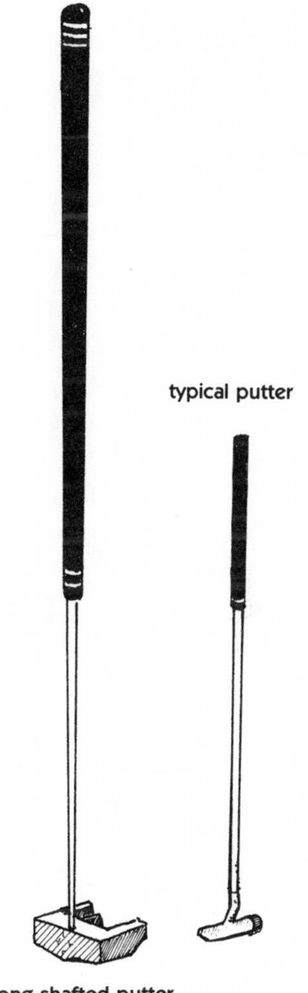

Another basic distinction involved the distribution of weight. Most putters are *heel-toe weighted,* with very little weight directly behind the ball. These are supposedly more resistant to twisting during off-center hits, and make it easier to keep the clubhead square throughout the stroke. *Blades, or flanged models,* generally have most of their weight behind the ball, and while they're not quite as forgiving, generally provide a cleaner, sleeker look than heel-toe weighted putters.

Extra-long putters are a recent trend. Sometimes over fifty inches long, the long putters allow the golfer to swing the club from a fixed point, providing a pure pendulum action. The end of the club is held under the chin with one hand, and the other hand pushes the club back and forth like a child on a swing. It has become popular among senior golfers because it allows them to putt without bending over and putting undue pressure on their backs.

Shafts

If you have to choose one thing to be knowledgeable about when it comes to golf clubs, choose shafts. Nothing is more important in selecting your new set of clubs than having the shaft fit your game and swing. You can have the finest made clubhead fit with the finest grip and even possess the finest swing—but if the shaft isn't the right flex for you, you won't hit a good shot.

It is somehow ironically appropriate that the most vital part of a golf club happens to be the most confusing part of the equipment industry. There are literally thousands of different shafts out there, made of different materials, all producing different results when combined with different clubheads. For that reason, shafts will always carry some mystery with them. But we will try to make the situation as clear as possible.

From the time that golf hit the shores of the United States in the late 19th century to the late 1930s, shafts were made primarily of hickory. Although the accepted standard for many years, hickory shafts had some serious shortcomings. Handmade from wood, they not only broke easily, but properties varied greatly from shaft to shaft. The biggest problem, however, was torque: Hickory is so supple that the shaft twisted a great deal during the swing, making it difficult to control the clubhead.

When steel shafts were introduced, they completely changed the face of not only the equipment industry, but of the golf swing, and of the game. The torque in a steel shaft is negligible, so the loose, floppy swing that compensated for the twisting of hickory immediately became outdated. A more athletic swing—one using the large muscles of the hips, back, and shoulders—was required. Players began hitting the ball significantly longer and straighter, and scores dropped. Today, steel remains the shaft of choice for most golfers. It's dependable, durable, and relatively inexpensive.

When you are talking about the characteristics of a steel shaft, you are speaking primarily of *flex.* Flex is the amount of bending a shaft will do during the swing, and the general rule is, the stronger you are, the stiffer your shaft should be. Steel shafts are available in a variety of flexes, from youth and ladies (very flexible) to extra stiff.

Okay, fundamentally it seems simple, but once you wander out into the marketplace, things get confusing. Some manufacturers label their shafts with letters ([L]adies, [R]egular, [S]tiff, [X]tra stiff, etc). Others assign numbers (1, 2, 3, 400, 500, etc). Still others combine letters and numbers. Add this to the fact that one manufacturer's stiff shaft may not be exactly the same flex as another manufacturer's stiff, and you might start to feel like you're getting the runaround.

Why the lack of standardization? The main reason is that manufacturers haven't agreed on one universal way to measure the flex of a shaft. Company A measures flex differently from Company B, so it's only logical that their flexes don't match up. It's an inconsistency that, unfortunately, the consumer can do little about, and precisely why it's so important to be equipment-educated before you go shopping for clubs.

It would be appropriate at this point to mention frequency-matching. "Frequency-matched shafts" is an exotic-sounding term you may hear thrown around in your local pro shop. It simply means that all the shafts in the set were tested by computer to make sure their flexes were precisely consistent club to club. The construction of a frequency-matched shaft is not necessarily any different than that of an unmatched shaft.

The other variable in the construction of steel shafts is the kick point, or the spot on the shaft where the greatest amount of flexing occurs during the swing. Some shafts have a *high kick point,* near the grip, which makes the club feel stiffer and produces a lower shot. Better players generally prefer a high kick point, something the Player and Bomber should keep in mind. A *lower kick point,* toward the clubhead, gives a more flexible feeling, and will help Thirtysomethings and Bunters get the ball airborne. Kick point can make quite a difference; in fact, you may not feel much difference between a stiff shaft with a low kick point and a regular shaft with a high kick point.

Graphite shafts surfaced briefly in the 1970s, but never caught on.

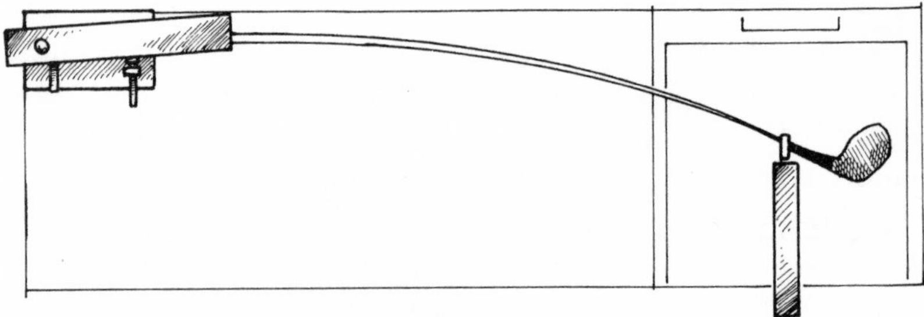

Shaft flex measured on a deflection board.

Limited production capabilities produced a primitive shaft that was lighter than steel, easier to swing, and promised increased clubhead speed and distance. However, the early graphite shafts had a high, unpredictable degree of torque and a record of breakage.

Industry advances resulting from years of trial and error have ignited graphite's comeback. Now, although a good deal more expensive than steel, graphite-shafted clubs are a pro shop staple. *Torque* is still an issue; in fact, it's the main concern among shaft manufacturers. For that reason, it needs to be one of your main concerns when shopping for graphite-shafted clubs. Generally, today's graphite shafts are available with a torque reading as low as two degrees and as high as seven. The higher the torque, the more the clubface will fan open on the backswing, and consequently, the more it will want to snap back to square, coming through impact. Golfers like The Player and The Bomber, who have no trouble with distance, will prefer a low-torque shaft that will provide reliable accuracy. Thirtysomethings and Bunters, for whom distance is a priority, will benefit from a higher torque shaft, perhaps five or six degrees, which provides that extra snap in the impact zone as the shaft twists back from open to square. Bananaballers, looking for a combination of more accuracy and distance, should settle somewhere in the middle, at about three or four degrees of torque.

Now, don't forget about flex; that's just as important. Graphite is a stiffer material than steel, but that doesn't mean a regular graphite shaft will be stiffer than a steel one. As a matter of fact, you really never know how stiff a shaft is going to be until you actually test the club. Manufacturers label their shafts in many different ways—some with words, like "soft," "ladies," "senior," "regular," "standard," "firm," or "stiff." Others use numbers, and still others, following the latest trend, label their shafts according to clubhead speed. That is, if you generate 90 mph of clubhead speed, you would choose the 87–96 mph shaft, 100 mph of clubhead speed, 97–106, and so on.

Graphite's composition allows it to be mixed with other materials to produce shafts with slightly different properties. Kevlar, the bulletproof plastic, is slightly softer than graphite, and when woven into a graphite shaft becomes a dampening agent, reducing the shock of off-center hits and providing a softer feel at impact. Boron, a lightweight but very expensive material, can be added to graphite to lighten and stiffen a shaft. Possessing incredible compressive strength, a layer of boron can replace three layers of graphite, reducing weight and adding strength. Boron was introduced to the golf industry in the 1970s to strengthen the breaking graphite shafts.

Another shaft material making an impact is titanium. Generally stiffer and more lightweight than steel with a high kick point, titanium has become a presence on the PGA Tour, where a stiff, lightweight shaft with almost no torque is a premium. Due to its limited properties, however, titanium remains a shaft fundamentally reserved for the stronger, more accomplished golfer.

Grips

The grip. It's just a piece of rubber, right? Not so fast. Since the grip is the only thing linking the club to your body, having a proper one at the end of the shaft is vital. What consitutes a proper grip? Size and comfort. The grip should be thin enough so that the fingertips of the left hand touch the heel of the hand when wrapped around the club, but not so thin that the nails dig in. Grips that are too thin force you to grip primarily with the fingers, leading to excessive hand action and inconsistent shots, whereas overly thick grips place the club in the palm, inhibiting the natural cocking and uncocking of the wrists and robbing you of power.

Comfort, of course, is a matter of individual taste, and to suit all the individuals out there, there are dozens of different grips available. Walk into a pro shop and you'll find most clubs fitted with the standard molded rubber grip. Others may have cord grips, which is a rubber grip molded with a coarse string folded in. Cord may be molded into the entire grip, or parts of it. The result is a rougher, livelier feeling in the hands.

Leather grips were the industry standard until the 1960s. When new, leather has a wonderfully soft feel, but it wears easily and doesn't stand up to moisture well. As a result, manufacturers have developed a waterproof rubber grip that closely resembles leather in look and feel. These "faux" leather grips have made an impact on Tour and are now infiltrating the marketplace.

Specialized grips? Super-soft, super-tacky, even grips made for arthritic hands are available. You'll rarely, if ever, find them standard issue with a set of clubs, but they can be ordered if so desired. Again, once the grip is the correct size for your hands, personal taste determines the "right" grip for you. What's most important is that the club doesn't slip in your hands.

Swingweight

Swingweight is another word you may hear tossed around the pro shop occasionally. It's important you know what it is, and what it isn't.

Swingweight refers to the distribution of weight in a golf club. Weight is deposited in the head end and the grip end of a golf club, and the relationship of those weights is the club's swingweight. It has nothing to do with overall weight. Two clubs may have the same overall weight, but if one of them has a greater ratio of weight in the head, it will feel heavier, and thus have a heavier swingweight.

Swingweight is measured in letter/number increments. Officially, the range is from A-0 to E-9; clubs in the "A" range have very little weight in the head (more in the grip) so they feel lightest. Conversely, clubs in the "E" range have most of their weight in the head and therefore feel heaviest. It's rare, however, that you'll find any sets outside of the C-4 to D-8 range. Beginning golfers, women, juniors, and seniors may prefer swingweights in the middle to high Cs, because the lighter feel makes it easier to create clubhead speed. Better and stronger players gravitate toward clubs in the low to mid Ds, which may give them a better sense of clubhead "feel." The standard for most men's clubs is D-0–2; for women, C-6–8.

Last But Not Least . . . Market Research

The final step in the education process is familiarizing yourself with the current market, so you can begin the buying process with a list of five or six models you think you want. Although it's not recommended to actually fit yourself for clubs at a golf discount house or warehouse (to be explained in the next chapter), it's a great place to browse and see what's available. You may even get a chance to test a few clubs on an indoor golf net. Resist any temptation you have to buy, however. There's more work to be done.

For the definitive word on what's new in the world of equipment, keep a close eye on the major golf magazines—*Golf Magazine, Golf Digest,* and *Golf World.* All three have a regular equipment column, as well as a yearly roundup sometime during the winter months. These "equipment bonanza" issues are valuable tools for the consumer. In addition to listing all models of all the major manufacturers, articles describe the latest and greatest equipment, who it's made for, and even how to use it. Being a magazine reader is the fastest and most effective way to become educated in the equipment industry.

FOUR

How To Buy the Right Way

Okay, you've studied all the facts. You know how a golf club is made. You can point to any part of any golf club and define it and its purpose. You know what your tendencies are as a golfer and what type of equipment is built for those tendencies. You know what's on the market, and you may even have an idea of what make and model you're interested in.

Don't think, however, that your new education qualifies you to pick up the nearest mail-order catalog and make an intelligent choice about a set of clubs. No one, no matter how much he or she knows about equipment, can do that.

Why? Simple: You don't know anything about a golf club until you've hit it.

Example: Club A is a forged cavity-back iron with an offset hosel and a graphite shaft, flex "standard." Sound like your kind of club? Well, sure, it may sound like "the one," it may look like "the one," but do you hear and see your ball around the golf course? You hit it, of course, and that is the bottom line. Club A seems, on paper, like the perfect match for you. But maybe its "offset" hosel is dramatically goosenecked. The club may in fact be less forgiving of off-center hits than you would prefer. It may make an annoying "ting" when contact is made. Who knows, you might just not like the way it feels in your hands. Remember what we said about graphite shafts? How one company's regular shaft can be the same as another company's stiff? What if this shaft turns out to be too stiff for you?

Another thing: Swinging a club is not nearly the same thing as hitting a ball with it, so don't make a decision based on how a club feels when you waggle it or make a few practice swings. Whatever you feel can be misleading. Take an example from the very halls of *Golf Magazine*. There are three five-irons that circulate from office to office, providing an outlet for frustrated editors who have written much more about golf than they have played it. Two are forged cavity-backed clubs with stiff steel shafts, and one is a cast club with a graphite shaft made for senior players. The senior club is without question the favorite club in the office. Why? Because it's lighter than the others, and easier to swing, and after sitting behind a desk for a few hours, who wants to make an effort swinging a club? If, however, any of the editors were fully warmed up and actually hit balls with the club, they would find the shaft to be too whippy and too light to feel controllable.

One more example: You spend Sunday watching Lenny Longballer win the PGA Tour's Three-Mile Island Open on TV. When asked about his stunning six-shot victory, Lenny shrugs off the effects of the radiation and attributes his success to his new driver, which, he says, has extra weight above the sweet spot, helping him to hit lower, more boring drives that are easier to control. Being a Bomber with wild, high-ball tendencies yourself, you scurry to the phone (along with thousands of other adoring TV viewers) and order a driver just like Lenny's. Well, not just like Lenny's. Lenny, being a pro, uses an extra stiff titanium shaft. You and your 17 handicap have always used a regular steel shaft. So, great, right? Your new driver is on the way, and along with it, your lower, more accurate tee shots.

Probably not. What you didn't think of is that a regular steel shaft will often have a low kick point, designed to hit the ball higher, which completely negates the lower trajectory features of the clubhead. The point here is that you can completely change the personality and performance of a club by changing just one of the components. You just never know until you actually hit it. What a shame it would be to discover these things after you've already committed yourself.

If this sounds a bit like playing the dating game, good: They're not dissimilar. Finding the right set of clubs is a good deal like finding the right mate. You may like the way someone looks and there may be some initial spark of attraction, but you really don't know if you can spend a lot of time with that person until you really get to know him or her. Have a few lunches. See a movie, perhaps. Compare high school yearbooks.

So how do you get to know a set of golf clubs? You hit them, of course! It's an absolutely vital, must-do step in the process of buying golf clubs. Its importance can't be stressed enough. In fact, it's the First Golden Rule of Buying Clubs:

> **Golden Rule #1:** YOU CAN'T MAKE AN INTELLIGENT CHOICE ABOUT CLUBS UNLESS YOU'VE HIT THEM FIRST.

Adhering to this rule narrows your options as far as where you can go in the search for your new set of clubs. We've already eliminated the mail-order route. Another resource you'll find ill-suited to your needs is the standard sporting goods store. Here you'll find a virtual supermarket of all kinds of sporting equipment, with a special section devoted to golf. In that section will be a salesperson possessing some knowledge of golf and equipment, but keep in mind that 1) almost never is he or she a PGA Professional, who would be trained in clubfitting; and 2) very rarely would you be given the opportunity to test the clubs. (If you did, it would likely be on an indoor range or a golf net, which makes an accurate analysis of your results impossible.) Furthermore, sporting goods stores are suspect when it comes to their equipment. Often you'll find last year's model on their racks, or a second-rate line at a low price for a quick sale to the beginning golfer. Which brings up the second Golden Rule of Buying Clubs:

> **Golden Rule #2:** SKILL LEVEL HAS NO CORRELATION TO QUALITY OF PRODUCT OR FIT. ALL PLAYERS SHOULD HAVE THE BEST EQUIPMENT POSSIBLE.

If you're a beginner, don't let anybody say you need anything but the finest-quality clubs available that are designed with the beginner's needs in mind. And don't ever, ever think that being a beginner means you don't need clubs that are precisely fit. The right clubs will help you learn the game and improve fastest. Ill-fitted clubs will do more to retard your progress than anything else.

You also want to beware of the large discount golf shops that have become popular. These stores carry just about everything associated with golf that you can imagine, including virtually every model of golf club on the market, all at a significantly discounted price. It's an alluring package. You walk in, the prices catch your eye, and you want to spend money. Try to control yourself. Although the selection, and perhaps the price, may be unparalleled, shopping at these stores still presents problems. Like a sporting goods store, usually little more than an indoor golf net is available for testing, and almost never will you find a PGA Professional on hand for testing. Instead, you'll be serviced by another "educated" salesperson, who may know plenty about what's available but likely knows little about clubfitting. The fact is, knowledge of equipment is secondary when it comes to clubfitting. Noted author and clubmaker Ralph Maltby explains:

> Most important in proper fitting of golf clubs is how knowledgeable the golf professional or other qualified person is regarding the swing itself, and then being able to translate each of the golfer's individual characteristics into proper equipment selection. The complications in proper fitting rise from matching the many possible combinations of golf clubs available with a particular golfer's swing and physical characteristics. To further complicate fitting, the golfer's potential must be evaluated from the standpoint of how his clubs will fit him later, should he have the desire or ability to substantially improve his golf game.[1]

So, see a PGA Professional. Indeed, you'd be best off at your own club, with a pro who knows your game. If you don't belong to a private club, see the pro at your local public course. All PGA Professionals, affiliated with public courses or private, have been trained in clubfitting. It's part of their education process.

That's not to say that all PGA Professionals are as attentive to clubfitting as they should be when it comes to selling equipment. You

---

[1]Maltby, Ralph. "Golf Club Design, Fitting, Alteration & Repair," p. 582.

may need to be a bit of a pusher and prodder to get the kind of service you need to ensure a complete clubfitting package.

What should you expect from your PGA pro? Well, let's start with the ideal. You won't get this kind of attention all the time, but it will give you an idea of how intensive the clubfitting process can be.

The last word in superpersonal, intensive clubfitting may very well come from golf professionals associated with the Henry-Griffets Golf Company. Henry-Griffets is a special manufacturer of golf clubs, a "custom" clubmaker. You cannot buy their clubs by mail. You cannot buy their clubs at a sporting goods store or at a discount house. Henry-Griffets clubs are only available through teaching professionals. But that's not what sets them—and the PGA professionals who sell Henry-Griffets—apart from the rest of the equipment industry.

What distinguishes Henry-Griffets and its staff of teaching professionals is the comprehensive fitting program. It's a system in which the consumer, teaching professional, and equipment manufacturer work together to find a set of golf clubs that best suits the consumer. And it's based on a belief that anyone in the market for golf clubs must remember, which is, coincidentally, The Third Golden Rule of Buying Clubs:

> **Golden Rule #3:** ONLY A TRAINED TEACHER OF THE GOLF SWING CAN ACCURATELY FIT A GOLFER TO A SET OF CLUBS. TEACHING AND FITTING GO HAND IN HAND.

Why? Consider the following example: Denny Divot, twelve handicapper, Bunting Bananaballer, goes to Billy Bob's Discount Golf Bonanza looking for a new driver. Billy Bob himself is working the floor and zeroes in on Denny, who complains that the ten-degree driver he now plays with hits the ball too high. Billy Bob smiles and leads Denny over to the barrel full of nine-degree drivers. "This'll give you those low screamers you're looking for," says Billy Bob, handing Denny a gleaming, graphite-shafted beauty. A hundred and fifty dollars later, Denny's on his way home.

But is he on his way to a better golf game? Dealing with Billy Bob, it's a crapshoot. On the other hand, with a teacher of the golf swing, i.e., PGA Professional, things are different. The first thing a pro might do is look at Denny's current driver. What Billy Bob never got to see is that there are marks all over the crown of Denny's club, indicating that the reason he hits the ball too high is because he's cutting under it, or popping it up. The next step is to take Denny out to the practice tee and see why he pops the ball up. What the pro can see (and what Billy Bob can't) is that Denny scoops at the ball through impact, leading to a choppy, up-and-down swing that often results in a pop-up. What the pro knows is that the scooping action is a compensation (and here's the irony) for the fact that Denny's driver *does not have enough loft,* so he is, albeit subconsciously, trying to help the ball in the air. What Denny really needs is a 12- or 13-degree driver that he can swing on a level path with the confidence that the ball will get airborne. The teaching professional was able to determine this by marrying his skills as a teacher with his knowledge of equipment. Billy Bob's analysis, in comparison, doesn't cut the mustard.

To ensure that the teaching professional produces under such circumstances, Henry-Griffets puts each and every pro in its program through a 4½-day clubfitting education school. There the pros learn how to coordinate their knowledge of the golf swing and basic clubfitting principles with Henry-Griffets' selection of 84 different clubs. That's right, 84. Different head models, different shaft flexes, torques, kick points, grips, lofts, lies, lengths—it adds up to 84 basic models of clubs. And that's just the basic models. One of the pros in the Henry-Griffets program tinkered with a few combinations and found that he could better service his members by offering 112 different clubs.

As frightening as 112 options may seem, the fitting process is not that complicated. The numbers are quickly narrowed once a profile of the golfer is established. Here's how a typical Henry-Griffets fitting session might go. We'll use our friend Denny again.

The teaching professional, having heard Denny's desire to purchase a new set of clubs, starts by asking a question. What's Denny's purpose? Why is he buying his new clubs? There's no right answer to this question, but the teaching professional has to know if the consumer is to get what he or she wants. Denny, for his part, wants to stop popping up his driver, get rid of his slice, and add ten more yards. Okay. Good answer, Denny!

The next step for the teaching professional is to get Denny to make a good, balanced swing, so both the teacher and Denny know what they're working toward—which is, by the way, a club that enables Denny to most often duplicate this motion.

The fitting process actually begins with something called an IMPACT BOARD. This is in big capital letters because it is an absolutely vital tool when it comes to properly fitting clubs. An impact board measures the lie of a golf club as it relates to the golfer. Lie was mentioned in Chapter 1. To refresh your memory, lie refers to the angle formed by the hosel of the clubhead and the ground when the clubhead

Impact board

is properly soled. If the lie is too upright, the toe of the club will be in the air and the clubface will point left, resulting in hooks. If the lie is too flat, the heel will be in the air, producing slices. Many manufacturers take lie into account when marketing clubs and, as a result, offer various combinations of flat, standard, and upright lies. However, too many club manufacturers feel that it is sufficient to determine a golfer's proper lie angle by putting a golf club in his or her hands and examining his or her address position. Not good. The toe of the club may sit half an inch above the ground at address, but that doesn't mean it's going to be at the same angle at impact. In fact, it's unlikely, which brings us to The Fourth Golden Rule of Buying Clubs:

> **Golden Rule #4:** THE ONLY LIE THAT COUNTS IS THE LIE AT IMPACT, AND IT CAN ONLY BE MEASURED WITH AN IMPACT BOARD.

Here's how it works: Denny hits several shots off a rigid wooden board. When the club hits the board, presumably at the same time as or just after impact, a mark is left on the sole of the club, the heel of the club is off the ground at impact, and the lie is too flat. If the mark is toward the heel of the club, the toe is off the ground at impact and the lie is too upright. If, however, the mark is in the middle of the sole, the lie suits the golfer and his or her swing.

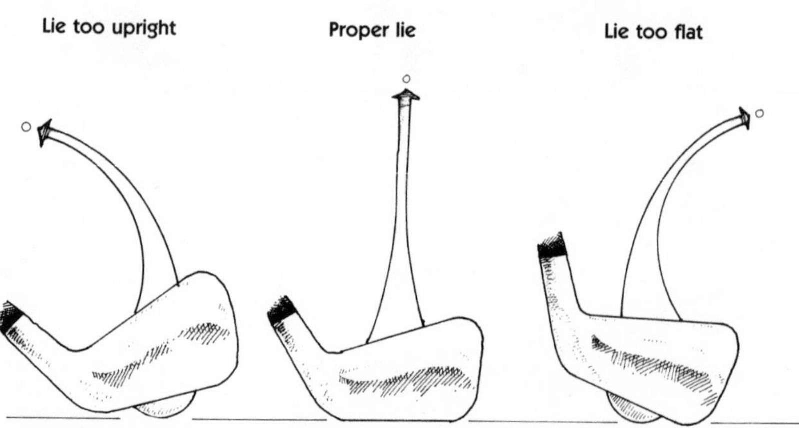

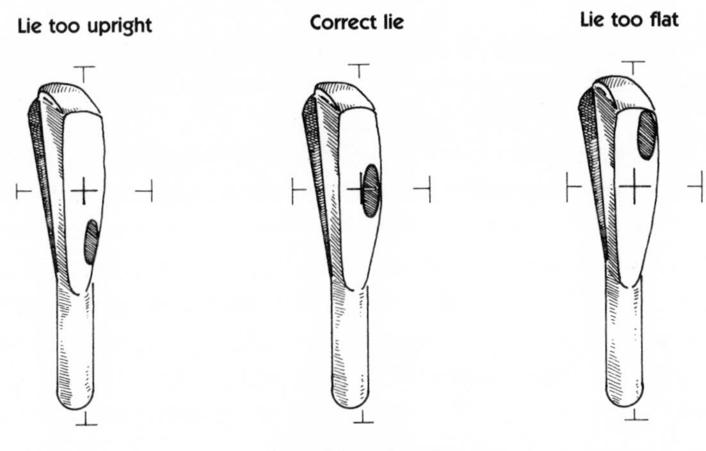

Impact board marks:

Once the proper lie is determined, the teaching professional concentrates on the shaft. By analyzing Denny's swing, shot patterns, and tendencies, as well as a process of trial and error, the pro determines what shaft flex best allows the student to perform at his or her peak. Often this can take some time, like trying to find the right frames at an optical shop. Pro and student may test six or seven different shafts before settling on one that seems best. And it's not always what either of them expect, either. Henry-Griffets has had Bombers opting for regular shafts and tiny little grandmothers choosing stiff, with full encouragement from their pro. Remember, the bottom line is finding the club that works best. Following so-called "rules" of various different equipment properties is not always the way to go. In fact, if there was an Unofficial Golden Rule of Buying Clubs, it might be this:

> **Unofficial Golden Rule:** OTHER THAN THE GOLDEN RULES, THERE ARE NO RULES.

Once a comfortable shaft flex has been determined, the pro analyzes Denny's shot trajectory and, again with some trial and error, determines the kick point that best suits him and his game. Various different swingweights are tested to find Denny's preference.

Based on personal taste, hand size, and strength, the pro and Denny choose a grip style and size. Another quick check on the impact board to make sure everything is shipshape, and Denny has his prototype golf club.

The process doesn't stop there. The Henry-Griffets teaching professional is also responsible for helping Denny determine the proper set makeup for his game and the courses he plays. Not all golfers are best served by three woods, ten irons, and a putter. Everybody's needs are different. The Henry-Griffets professional has no problem outfitting Denny with ten woods and three irons, if it is more suitable to his game. We will take an in-depth look at set makeup later in the book. It's important to realize now, however, that like everything else in clubfitting, it's not a foregone conclusion.

The specs are sent to Henry-Griffets, and the clubs are delivered within a few weeks.

Chances are you've never heard of Henry-Griffets before. It's also not unreasonable to think that there might not be a Henry-Griffets professional in your area. That's okay. The purpose of the last few pages was not to sell you on their clubs. It was to show you how intensive a precise fitting process can be, and to point out that there is at least one equipment manufacturer that sees the necessity in being that thorough when it comes to clubfitting.

So we've proved a point, but where does that leave you, the consumer? Yes, if you can find a Henry-Griffets professional in your area, it's worth a call. But that doesn't mean that every pro who isn't on the Henry-Griffets staff isn't a painstaking clubfitter. Some certainly are. You ought to have an idea of what an independent pro can and should do for you when you go to him or her for a set of clubs.

Okay. You've done all your research and you've come up with several different sets of clubs that you think fit the needs of your golf game and budget. You walk into the pro shop of your private course, local public track, or driving range, and you announce to the PGA Professional that you're in the market for a new set of clubs. First thing to do: Book a lesson, even two or three. Even if the pro is familiar with your game, give him or her an opportunity to give your swing a second look with regard to clubfitting.

Once you've had your lesson and the pro has become acquainted (or reacquainted) with your game and needs, it's back to the pro shop. Give the pro a list of clubs you're interested in. He or she may not have all, or even any, of those clubs in stock, but ask the pro to give an honest opinion on those clubs' compatibility with your game. It's important to know if your initial choices were good ones, because things get complicated if they're not available.

The pro will say something like, "Sorry, Denny, I don't carry Brand X. But Brand Y is basically the same thing. Why don't you have a look at these?" Don't panic. In most cases, the pro is right; but you need to beware of one possibility: the bulk/clone ploy.

The bulk/clone ploy is a money-making opportunity for the professional that, unfortunately, does not have the consumer's best interests at heart. Here's the way it works: Say Brand X is an enormously popular golf club, so popular that the plant is riddled with back orders and the professional can't get his or her hands on any to sell. However, Brand Z, a Brand X clone, is readily available, and at a fraction of the cost. A couple of catches, though. Brand Z is so inexpensive because, although it looks a lot like Brand X, it's not as well made. It's also a good possibility that Brand Z is only available to the professional in bulk, so although he or she can buy a set of clubs for relatively little and sell them with a big markup, he has to move many sets for the bulk/clone ploy to pay off. As a result, the professional will be pushing Brand Z whenever possible. It's the quickest opportunity to make money.

This is where your market knowledge will help. Having studied the equipment issues of all the golf magazines, you'll know something is a little strange if the alternative offered to you is a name you've never heard of. If you're not sure, make a note of what else is in stock, tell him or her you'll be back, and go home. Refer back to your magazines and check if 1) Brand Z is legitimate; and 2) if the other clubs you saw in the shop are compatible with your game. If Brand Z is a knockoff and you are on the verge of becoming a victim of the bulk/clone ploy, you have two options: Go back and tell the pro you're only interested in clubs you've researched (if the pro has any), or, go elsewhere. You've spent money on a lesson, but that is never money wasted, even if you didn't get a set of clubs out of the deal. So the Fifth Golden Rule of Buying Clubs is a bit of *caveat emptor:*

Golden Rule #5: BEWARE OF THE BULK/CLONE PLOY AND OTHER COVERT MANEUVERS THAT AREN'T AIMED AT YOUR BEST INTERESTS.

If, on the other hand, Brand Z is legitimate, or, even better, the pro carries some or all of the clubs you have on your list, it's time to move on to the next step: testing and fitting.

Remember the First Golden Rule: You can't make an intelligent decision about clubs unless you hit them first. The professional should either have demo sets of the model you're interested in, or should let you test the clubs right off the rack. If the pro is hesitant about letting you do that, assure him or her that you are serious about making a purchase. If the pro still won't let you test the clubs, take your business elsewhere. A professional who won't let you test the clubs you're interested in is not only fouling up your fitting process, but also is not doing his or her job.

In a perfect world, the pro measures your clubhead speed on a special computerized swing analyzer to determine the proper shaft flex. The pro has an impact board to find the right lie angle. The pro has the club you're looking for in several different lengths to test on a trial-and-error basis. He or she has different shaft flexes, different swing-weights, different grip sizes—every conceivable option for you to try to find the specifications that fit you perfectly. Of course, unless the clubs you're looking for are Henry-Griffets, it's unlikely he or she is going to have such a complete setup. Chances are the pro won't have the expensive swing analyzer, or clubs of various lengths and swing-weights. He or she might not even have a great selection of shaft flexes. It's a tough position for the consumer, but you have to make do.

The club professional should, however, join you for the testing process. He should watch you hit each club, not only keeping an eye on the results (where the ball goes) but also on which club allows you to make the best pass at the ball. The pro should have you hit shots from an impact board to determine the proper lie. Don't skimp here; ask for an impact board before you take your first lesson. If he or she doesn't have one, and doesn't have the time or resources to make one, you can actually make one yourself. A simple piece of plywood will do: about 4 x 5 feet, large enough so you can stand on the board in street shoes and assume your normal address position with a 5-iron. Make sure you use it on level ground, preferably cement, so it lies perfectly flat. A really precise pro will bring along a box of lead tape (one piece = one swingweight) so you can experiment with different swingweights.

As for specifications such as shaft flex, torque, length, and loft, odds are the professional won't have any of the machinery needed to give the answers. The pro will have to rely on personal knowledge of the golf swing and how it relates to equipment, and, well, that's okay. After all, that's sort of what the pro's job is all about. If such a subjective, nonscientific approach makes you uneasy, don't be afraid to ask questions. What is it about your trajectory that leads the pro to believe you need stiff shafts? Would thinner grips help? Why less torque instead of more? Go ahead and ask. Remember, you're planning to give him or her your money. You're certainly within your rights.

By the end of the session, the professional should have made a list of the specifications that fit your game and swing. If you're lucky, all your specs will be standard and you'll be able to pull a set of clubs off the rack and put them in your bag. If not, the pro will order your clubs directly from the manufacturer. Delivery time is generally slow. Don't let that deter you from holding out for properly fit clubs.

You've probably gathered by now that the level of precision in your fitting session is almost completely dependent on the professional and his or her policies and practices. It's true, and unfortunately, most pros can make a decent buck on their equipment without being very thorough clubfitters; the reason being, of course, that most consumers are either willing to or don't know that they shouldn't, settle for less than complete service. You, on the other hand, know what it takes to be an intelligent consumer, and although you're probably not going to change the way a professional sells and fits clubs, you can make sure the service you receive is adequate.

Lay everything out before you start with the pro. Say, "I want to buy a new set of golf clubs. I'd like to start by taking a lesson or two—

which I'll pay you for—then test a few clubs I'm interested in. I'd like you to join me for the testing process and help me make an intelligent choice. And I'd like to use an impact board to make sure we've got the right lie. When can we schedule this?" The pro will probably respect you for your knowledge and thoroughness. If for some reason he or she doesn't agree to this, look elsewhere until you find someone who will. It's important that your clubfitter know exactly what you want before you start the process. It will make it easier for you both.

FIVE

Getting the Combination Right

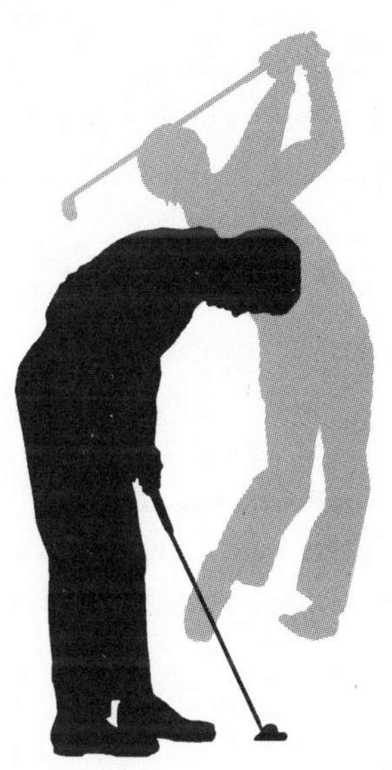

Okay, so you've found your dream set of golf clubs. You love the way they look, the shafts are right for you, the grips feel great, and above all, they performed well when you hit them. Now, here's your next dilemma: The Rules of Golf say you're allowed to carry up to fourteen clubs at a time, including a putter. How would you like them? Three woods and eight irons, or three and nine? How about two woods and nine irons? We could do four and nine, or grab a 1-iron and do two and 11.

Combinations. They're important in buying golf equipment, because if you get the wrong combination of golf clubs in your bag, you'll find yourself out on the course with a couple of clubs you never hit and wishing you could hit some others that you don't have.

For example, if the Thirtysomething buys 11 irons, he or she is going to learn quickly that he or she has a lot of trouble hitting the 1, 2, and 3-irons, and is going to stop using them. But, because the Thirtysomething only has one fairway wood (most likely the 3-wood, no bowl of cherries in itself), he or she will drop all the way down to a 4- or 5-iron for long shots from the fairway and rough. And that won't be enough club. The Thirtysomething spent all that money on a set of clubs that fit perfectly, only to use two-thirds of them.

For the sake of your game as well as your wallet, be prudent when it comes to selecting the combination of clubs you wish to put in your bag. It's not always easy. To give you some ideas, here are a few sample sets that might be appropriate for our group of five golfers. Remember, these are only suggestions, by no means etched in stone. You never know what you'll find after you go through the testing process.

Thirtysomethings

11-degree driver, 3, 4, 5, 7 woods, oversized metal or graphite heads, mid- to high-torque graphite shafts. 4 - 9 irons, PW, SW, investment-cast, perimeter-weighted with mid- to high-torque graphite shafts, regular flex putter.

The logic behind this set makeup is that woods are easier to hit than long irons, especially oversized metalwoods. Take out the 1-, 2-, and 3-irons, replace them with the 4-, 5-, and 7-woods, and you've got a practical, playable set of golf clubs. Metalwoods have more perimeter-weighting than irons, so they make it easier to get balls into the air and are more forgiving of off-center hits, of which there will be plenty. Irons have investment-cast, perimeter-weighted heads for maximum forgiveness. A good deal of sole-weighting is recommended to help get the ball up. The four-iron, which straddles the line between long- and mid-iron, has enough loft that it shouldn't present too much of a problem for the beginning golfer. We've added graphite shafts in all clubs, save the putter, to lighten the overall weight and increase clubhead speed for maximum distance.

Bananaballer

2-wood, or driver with 12–13 degrees loft, metal or graphite heads, 3, 5, 7 woods. Steel shafts, regular flex (mid-torque graphite optional). 4 - 9 irons, investment-cast, perimeter-weighted, steel shafts, regular flex (mid-torque graphite optional). PW, SW, LW, putter. Grips 1/16 inch undersized (optional).

There are a couple of rules at work here to remember: The less loft, the easier it is to slice; and, long irons are easier to slice than fairway woods. Instead of choosing a standard driver (7–11 degrees of loft), the bananaballer would be better with a higher-lofted club for the tee shot, such as a 2-wood. With more loft, sidespin and thus slicing is reduced. Less spin is produced by metal and graphite heads, so we've eliminated the option of wood. To take advantage of the forgiveness of perimeter-weighting, the long irons are replaced with 5- and 7-woods. They're not only more forgiving but easier to hit from the rough, a familiar place to the bananaballer. The irons have investment-cast, perimeter-weighted heads to maximize correction of off-center hits. A third, or lob wedge, is also added. A slicer doesn't hit many greens in regulation, which puts pressure on his short game to help him compete. A lob wedge with 60 degrees of loft or more will add a needed extra dimension to his game around the greens. To eliminate the torque factor, we've recommended steel shafts in a regular flex. Graphite shafts are also okay, as long as careful attention is paid to the torque level. Too much torque may make straightening out that slice difficult. Something else to think about is the undersized grips, which will put the grip more in the fingertips, increasing hand action.

Bunter

1, 3, 5, 7 woods, metal or graphite heads, regular, high-torque graphite shafts. 3 - 9 irons, investment cast, perimeter-weighted, OR forged cavity-backed, regular, high-torque graphite shafts. PW, SW, putter. Grips 1/32 undersized (optional).

The 5- and 7-woods might well be the most important clubs in this golfer's bag. Repeatedly faced with longer shots into the greens because of modest length off the tee, the Bunter will appreciate the consistency and for giveness of the high-lofted fairway woods. The 7-wood, or "utility" wood, is easier to get balls airborne, from the fairway and the rough, than the long, thin blade of a long iron. The three-iron may even be dropped in favor of a third wedge. Since the Bunter is ordinarily a consistent ball-striker, forged clubs should be considered. But because he cannot afford the dropoff in distance that will result from a mis-hit with a traditional blade, the Bunter should stick to a cavity-backed head, which is more forgiving. Shafts in all clubs are high-torque graphite, regular flex, which will provide plenty of kick through impact for maximum distance. Like the Bananaballer, the Bunter may benefit from thinner grips, which increase hand action, and, potentially, clubhead speed.

Bomber

1, 4 woods, metal or graphite heads, steel shaft, stiff flex. 3 - 9-irons, investment-cast, perimeter-weighted, steel shaft, stiff flex. PW, SW, LW(60), LW(64).

A crusher of the golf ball does not need a vast array of long clubs. A 4-wood will perform adequately from virtually any lie in the fairway, and if the lie in the rough is dicey, this player has enough strength to slash it out with the 3-iron. When accuracy off the tee becomes a problem, the 4-wood provides a nice blend of accuracy and power. Woodheads are made of metal or graphite, to reduce spin. Irons have investment-cast, perimeter-weighted heads, offering maximum forgiveness of the inconsistencies characteristic of the Bomber's swing. The weakest part of a long hitter's game, generally, is around the green. This set makeup focuses on that shortcoming. By adding a third and fourth wedge of varied lofts, the Bomber can hit a variety of different short shots without having to manipulate his or her swing for different distances. Stiff-flexed steel shafts are in all clubs for consistency and control.

Player

1, 3, 5 (utility) woods, wood, metal, or graphite, steel or low-torque graphite shafts, stiff flex. 1 – 9 irons, forged, traditional blades or cavity-backed, steel or low-torque graphite shafts, stiff flex. PW, SW, LW(60), LW(64).

Hey, wait a second! That makes seventeen clubs! That's three too many!

Sure it is, but it doesn't mean that they should all be in the bag at the same time. The Player's game is refined enough that different days call for different set makeups. For example, on a long, hilly course, a

5-wood and a third wedge might be added in favor of the 1- and 2-irons, because the long irons are difficult to hit from sidehill lies, and elevated greens make chips and pitches a bit more complicated. On the other hand, on a tight, tree-lined course, the 1-iron becomes an invaluable commodity off the tee. The Player also has the luxury of being good enough to play any club. The Player will gravitate toward forged blades, however; cavity-backs if he or she is looking for a little insurance against mis-hits. He or she will like stiff steel or low-torque graphite shafts for their consistency, and the Player will want to have options on hand. Investing in a few extra clubs is worth it, as long as every club you own can be used to your advantage at some time, in some way.

The Pros

If you made your living playing golf, and you had your choice of any clubs you wanted, what would you arm yourself with? Interesting question, isn't it? With so many options out there, what do the best players in the world, who count on their equipment to help them put food on their tables, put in their bags?

It's also a worthwhile question to answer. You'd be surprised at the lengths a PGA Tour professional will go to make sure he or she is comfortable with the sticks he or she is swinging. Pros are extremely picky when it comes to clubs, and most will claim to be so equipment-sensitive that they can tell if a set is as little as a degree off from their specifications. At a tour event in Florida, a leading pro sent his caddy—and his sand wedge—to the trailer of the equipment manufacturer he was under contract with. "Tell 'em to make it fifty-six, and I mean fifty-six," he told his caddy, referring to the loft. "I told 'em last week and I think it's sitting at about fifty-five now."

This may seem a little fanatical to the average golfer, but it's an indication of how important properly fitted clubs are. There could have been a number of reasons why that Tour pro was so insistent on a fifty-six-degree sand wedge. Maybe the bunkers at that course were exceptionally steep. Perhaps the fairways were cut a bit longer, reducing backspin and calling for higher, softer-landing shots.

So, you'll find all sorts of interesting specifications in the pros' bags. They've had their clubs "tweaked" so they look, feel, and perform just the way they want. Sometimes the "recipes" for success will surprise you. For example, almost every pro on Tour, whether he or she hits it long or short, carries a driver with an X (extra-stiff) shaft. Makes sense for Mark Calcavecchia, one of the Tour's longballers. But why would Larry Mize, one of the Tour's shortest hitters, play with X shafts? Mize is also one of the straightest hitters on Tour, which may be an explanation. He sacrifices a few yards for precious accuracy. Another trend on tour is high swingweights. Most pros' drivers are in the D-4 to D-7 range, well above the standard D-2 you'll find in the pro shops. A high swingweight means the weight is balanced farther toward the head of the club. Pros like Hal Sutton (D-7) like that because it gives them a better feel for the clubhead, although, again, clubhead speed, and therefore distance, become more of an effort. Low drives are a premium on Tour: They fight the wind better, hold their line better, and roll when they land. As a result, most drivers on Tour have less loft than the industry standard of eleven degrees. Raymond Floyd's driver is 8.5 degrees. Hale Irwin's is 10 degrees. Curtis Strange, a naturally high-ball hitter, carries a 7 degree driver in an effort to keep it low.

The pros are also very particular when it comes to set makeup, or the combination of clubs they carry. For them, it's like a football coach putting the eleven players on the field who best match up with the opponents. Raymond Floyd credits part of his 1976 Masters victory to the addition of a 5-wood to his bag. He dropped his 2-iron, and found that he was more effective attacking Augusta National's par-5s with the 5-wood. You'll find an abundance of fairway woods common among the shorter hitters on the PGA Tour, as well as most players on the senior PGA and LPGA tours. Like the average amateur, they find 4- and 5-woods easier to hit and control than one- and 2-irons. There's a lesson to be learned here: Fred Couples is a big, strong man and carries a one-iron. Corey Pavin is no less of a golfer but somewhat smaller in size and carries a 4-wood instead. Now, be smart: Who are you going to emulate?

The same goes for components. Dave Love spent a few months in

1993 with graphite shafts in his irons. He claimed that they reduced the shock in his hands, allowing him to practice more. This is a guy who hits hundreds of balls every day, so wear and tear on his wrists and hands is a concern. Is it for you? Probably not, when you consider that a whimsical switch to graphite is going to cost you hundreds of dollars. Davis got his shafts for free.

Tour pro Tom Sieckmann plays with one of the most unusual set makeups on tour. He carries four wedges, with lofts of 50, 54.5, 59, and 64.5 degrees. Four different wedges give him a wider variety of shots from 100 yards and in without changing his swing. Being a long hitter, Sieckmann faces these "touch shots" often, so he packs his bag accordingly. To stay under the 14-club limit, he dropped his 3- and 5-irons. It's an unorthodox system, yet the average golfer would do well to play with a similar arrangement of clubs. The quickest way to lower your scores is to improve your short game, and making wedges a priority is a good start.

Ask the pro at your course to reshaft a club and it will likely be weeks or even months before you see it again. On Tour, however, there's no time to waste. Equipment manufacturers have giant trailers on site at each tournament. These trucks are stocked to the gills with clubheads, every kind of grip and shaft imaginable, and all kinds of maintenance and repair equipment. They're traveling pro shops that can reshaft a player's clubs and have them ready the next morning. Players have an opportunity to experiment with different combinations, which leads to some interesting set makeups. Take Bob Eastwood, for example, who has steel shafts in his mid- and short-irons but had his 2- through 4-irons fitted with graphite, which, he found, produced a higher trajectory. For the same reason, Peter Persons did the same thing, except he chose titanium.

With the equipment trailers there every week, the average Tour player's bag is in a constant state of evolution. Each week it's a different golf course, with different weather conditions. Needs change. At the Masters, for example, persimmon drivers are prevalent. They're softer and more playable than metal, allowing the pros to work the ball around Augusta National's famous doglegs. When the Tour makes its swing through Texas, windy conditions are prevalent, so the trailers are beseiged with requests for 7 and 8 degree drivers that will keep the ball down. Wet days call for higher-lofted drivers that will carry the ball further to compensate for the roll they won't get. When the Tour stops at a long course, utility woods—clubs with the loft of a 4 or 5-wood and perhaps a rail on the sole—become popular, because they're more effective than long irons. They even match putters to the course they're playing. Tom Kite has five putters with five different lofts, however minute. The longer the grass on the greens that week, the more lofted putter he uses. You don't need to be quite that fanatical, but think about the course you play and the conditions you play under. In this case, the pros' preferences usually apply to you, too.

SIX

Women, Seniors, Juniors, and Lefties

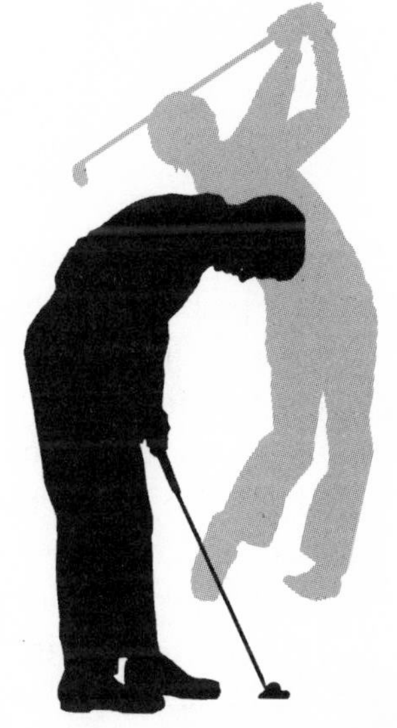

"Someday," says Tom Galvin of the PGA of America, "golf clubs will be genderless and ageless. There will just be a large selection of components, and any golfer, young, old, male, or female, will be able to choose those components that fit him or her best."

How nice it would be if Mr. Galvin's prediction came true: Everybody would have clubs that fit. In the meantime, however, golf clubs are, for the most part, made for one type of person. The reality of the situation is, unfortunately, this: If you're not a man of middle age or younger, you are a second-class citizen in the world of golf equipment. Women, seniors, juniors, and left-handed golfers are, on the whole, thrown crumbs of attention while men get the entire loaf. Companies that manufacture eight models of men's clubs will perhaps offer two ladies' models and one junior set. Senior clubs are even rarer. Left-handed clubs are available, but often not in every model, and if you are unfortunate enough to be a left-handed woman, senior, or junior, the outlook gets bleaker. As a result, most lefties learn to play with right-handed clubs. You won't see a proliferation of these "other" clubs when you walk into the standard pro shop. Even at the big discount warehouses, the selection of clubs for "other" golfers is slim compared to the "in" crowd, the men. The explanation for this, of course, is the old rule of supply and demand: Fewer women, juniors, seniors, and lefties play golf than right-handed men, so fewer buy clubs. Why make and carry clubs that aren't going to sell?

It's tough to argue with that, but still, those of you who fit into that "other" category must be able to find clubs that fit.

Women

Walk into the pro shop, and if you see fifteen sets of men's clubs on the racks, you'll probably see four or five sets of clubs made for women. They're shorter, have more flexible shafts, and, unfortunately, are usually adorned with overly precious pink or baby blue trim. Often the models will be chosen randomly, with little thought given to representing different skill levels. For that reason, you must be even more particular when it comes to your fitting session. The most important thing is that you come away from the experience with a set of specifications that describes the right clubs for you. Don't allow yourself to be fitted to one of the sets in the professional's shop unless it truly fits. If one of the sets of clubs in the shop seems perfect, then by all means buy it, but don't feel like you have to make a purchase at this particular shop. If you're going about this correctly, you're already paying the professional for at least one lesson, so don't worry about wasting his or her time.

So what if you don't feel comfortable with any of the clubs available? You may very well not; not all women need shorter or even more flexible shafts. You're going to have to take your chances and go elsewhere. You've got your list of specifications (shaft flex, length, lie angle, loft, swingweight). Now go find some clubs you like, and make sure they can be altered to fit your specifications, if necessary. Keep in mind that the casting process makes irons more difficult to adjust. Remember Golden Rule #1: You can't make an intelligent choice about a club unless you hit it (even if the specs are perfect!)

Seniors

Manufacturers are beginning to wise up with respect to the over-50 crowd. Demographics tells them that the real spenders are between 25 and 45 years of age, but the average age of America's golfer is near 50.

Although seniors, as a group, may not be as quick to open their billfolds as the young movers and shakers, they make up an enormous part of the game, and deserve to be noticed. As a result, more and more manufacturers are offering clubs designed specifically for the senior golfer: softer, longer shafts designed to increase clubhead speed and distance, more loft to get the ball up, and perimeter weighting for forgiveness of off-center hits. Oversized heads with larger sweet spots have become a senior favorite. Sometimes long irons are eliminated in favor of higher-lofted fairway woods or extra wedges.

But this is all fairly new; for years, senior players have had to make do with regular clubs, watching their games deteriorate as their strength and flexibility diminished. Now, there are more options, but that doesn't mean that they are well represented in the pro shops. A typical selection of senior clubs in a shop is not quite as good as that of the ladies. As America's golfers grow older in the next few years, that may change, but in the meantime, a more likely alternative is this: Go through the fitting process, get your specs, then make a custom order of a men's model. You may want a more flexible shaft, or a particular set makeup. Perhaps just thinner grips are all you need. In any case, you can get clubs that fit you. Just be thorough about the clubfitting process.

Juniors

Nobody presents more of a clubfitting challenge than an avid junior golfer. As a parent, you want to get your child a set of clubs that will best help him or her learn and improve, but you don't want to spend hundreds of dollars on a set of clubs if they're not going to fit the child in six months. Growth spurts can be awfully expensive. And what if the child is just taking up the game? An entire set of clubs seems a bit extreme, doesn't it? So what's the smart move?

The PGA of America has devoted a lot of time to this subject. Children are the future of golf, so it's important that they are introduced to the game properly. Manufacturers have similarly sentimental feelings, so most of them offer a junior set. Most are comprised of one or two woods and 4 - 5- irons and a putter, and cost a few hundred dollars.

They are classified as being suitable for ages 5–14, or 5–9, or 10–14, or what have you, and they make nice Christmas gifts.

Problem is, they're not easy to find. Most professionals will have catalogs from which they can order junior sets, but you won't always find the actual clubs in the shop because people aren't pounding on the doors to buy junior clubs. It's part of a larger problem; golf is an expensive sport, so not enough children are getting into the game; those who do are usually presented with a set of men's or ladies' clubs that have been cut down to fit. Cut-down clubs: A time-honored tradition. So what about them? Is that okay for your child?

Only to a small extent. If your child is just taking up golf, not really sure whether it's a game he or she could spend a lot of time playing, cutting down a couple of clubs (maybe a wood, short iron, and putter) is a fine idea. It gives them something they can whack the ball around with until they decide to take the game more seriously. Remove the grip (see regripping, p. 79), cut the shaft with a tube cutter from your local hardware store, and then put on a new grip (p. 80). If the child is really small, the shaft may be too short for a grip. Athletic tape will do.

Once the child has decided to play regularly, cut-down clubs become a problem. Cutting down an adult club not only makes the shaft stiffer and inappropriate for juniors, but throws off the balance point and swingweight as well. It's like giving somebody a poorly designed club and asking him or her to learn the game with it. Inevitably the golfer will build compensations into his swing, leading to ingrained faults that will be difficult to fix when there is an opportunity to use well-made clubs.

The solution? You might have guessed it by now: Go see your PGA Professional, and make sure the pro has made some commitment to junior golf by stocking the appropriate equipment. If it's not there, go elsewhere.

Have your son or daughter spend some quality instructional time with the pro, working on swing and testing various sets of clubs. The standard junior set may fit perfectly; perhaps a women's set is a more appropriate option. You never know until your child has a chance to test the clubs.

The ideal, although perhaps unrealistic, is to put your child through a Henry-Griffets-type fitting program where he or she is not fitted for "junior clubs" per se, but a component makeup that simply reflects physical build and ability level at the time. This gets costly during the growing years. If you're willing to pay the price, your child will be best equipped to learn the game properly and make the fastest progress toward excellence.

As for the problem of growth, there are several things you can do. One thing you shouldn't do is buy clubs that are far too long for your child in anticipation of him or her growing into them. By the time the clubs fit, the swing faults will be so plentiful that your child will probably want to give up the game. What you can do is have your child undergo periodic fitting sessions to make sure the clubs still fit. If the shafts are too short, they can be lengthened at considerably less cost than a new set of clubs. If your child has grown too strong for the shaft in the clubs, it's probably a better idea to buy a new set rather than reshaft the old set. The difference in cost is not that much.

You can also ask your pro about leasing demo sets, which would allow your junior to play with, say, a set of ladies' clubs, then return them when the season's over and wait and see how much growth occurs during the winter.

So, until Tom Galvin's dream of genderless, ageless golf clubs comes true, finding clubs for those "other" people means you just have to work a little more, look a little harder, and be a little more patient.

SEVEN

Putters

Probably the most important thing you should know about buying a putter is that Arnold Palmer has 3,000 of them. Why? So he can switch when the particular one he's using stops "working." Because for Arnie and every other golfer in the world, there is one golden rule of putters: The best-made putter in the world is the one that sinks putts for you that day.

It's a completely different game from the rest of golf. Walk along the practice tee at a PGA Tour event and you'll have problems identifying a certain pro from his swing. There are certain rules of physics and gravity that make most swings look fundamentally alike. On the putting green, however, there's only one rule: Get the ball in the hole. As a result, at any given Tour event you'll see a veritable cornucopia of some very distinct putting styles. Bobby Locke will always be known for his hooking stroke. Jack Nicklaus' characteristic crouch over the ball has been emulated by amateurs for years. Raymond Floyd stands very tall with almost no crouch. Paul Azinger uses a funny grip and a short, popping stroke. Ben Crenshaw uses a traditional grip and a long, flowing stroke. Tom Kite putts with a cross-handed grip. All are fantastic putters.

All use different putters, as well—tools that they have found to be ideally suited to their style. Crenshaw probably wouldn't feel comfortable using Azinger's putter, and it's certain Nicklaus would have a hard time crouching over Floyd's extra-long flatstick.

The moral of this story is that there's no absolute, etched-in-stone, "right" way to putt, so there's no rule that says putter X is going to be any more suitable for you than putter Y. For that reason, the selection of putters on the market is great. There are popular models of putters, to be sure, and there are a couple that you'll find on Tour in double digits, but the bottom line is, if you putt well with it, it's the right putter for you. Pros take this philosophy to the extreme: Compare Palmer's fair-weather attitude with Gary Player, who has used the same putter for his entire career.

You probably can't afford to go the Palmer route, but you don't have to emulate Player, either. You never know how and when your preferences are going to change. On fast greens you might prefer a light, blade-type putter. On slower greens you may feel more comfortable with a heavier, mallet-headed putter. Or, for that matter, vice versa. Putters come with big heads, small heads, offset hosels, standard hosels, heel-toe weighted, blades, long shafts, short shafts, heavy, light, brass, steel, graphite, kevlar, the list goes on and on.

Try a few putters. As with other clubs, avoid the sporting goods store and discount golf house. Go to a golf course where you can test the putters on an actual green. Find one that you like to look at, that feels good in your hands, and above all, that you putt relatively well with. If you sour on it after a year or so, you can always buy another one. It doesn't mean you have to trash the first putter; chances are you'll want to go back to it eventually. Think of it as buying a suit: It's always good to have a variety of options.

EIGHT

Balls, Bags, and Other Pets

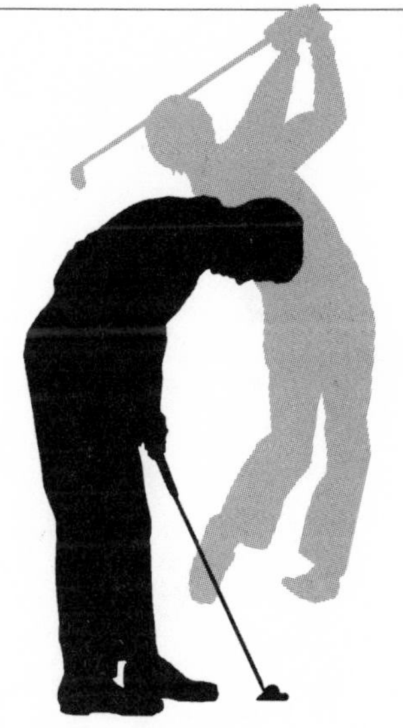

Ah, accessories. What would your golf clubs do without them? Not much. You need a bag to carry them in, balls to hit, shoes, and gloves, to mention a few necessities. Here's how to be smart about properly outfitting yourself.

Balls

Ever see an ad for tennis balls in which the company claims their balls bounce higher than any other? Or an ad for basketballs guaranteeing the ball will fly straighter?

The reason this sounds a bit ridiculous is because, for the most part, a tennis ball is a tennis ball and a basketball is a basketball. As long as they're round and bouncy, everything's fine.

In golf, however, the object is to hit your ball farther and straighter than the next player, so manufacturers compete to make "the best ball": one that flies longer, fights the wind better, and stops quicker when landing on the green. The market is filled with hundreds of different balls, all claiming properties that outdo the competition. How do you make a choice?

It's tough. But a basic idea of the different types of golf balls available will make it easier. Let's start with the two basic types: two-piece "solid" balls, and three-piece "wound" balls.

Two-piece balls are made by covering a high-energy rubber ball with durable plastic called surlyn. Two-piece surlyn balls spin less, roll longer, and are resistant to scuffing and cutting.

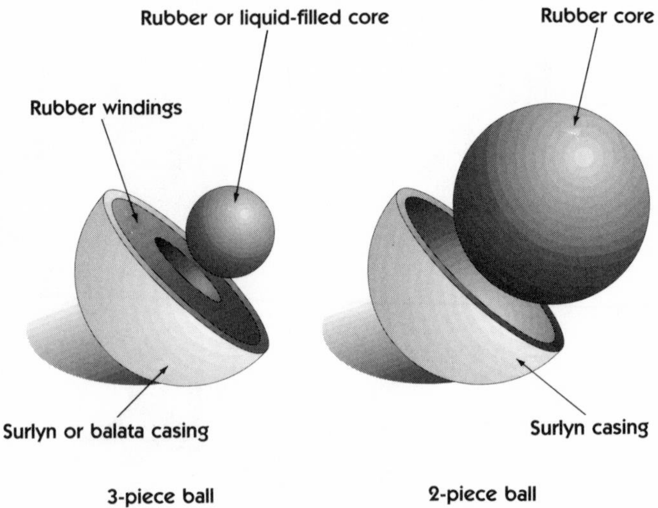

Three-piece balls are made by wrapping rubber windings around a solid rubber or liquid-filled core, then encasing it in a cover made of either surlyn, or balata, a soft rubber. Although balata balls cut and scuff easily, they have a softer feel and spin faster, producing quick stops on the greens, and are preferred by better players. Wound surlyn balls are more durable, yet have a softer feel and more spin than a two-piece surlyn ball, thus appealing to the better golfer looking for a bit more durability. Three-piece balls are available in various compressions. The higher the compression, the greater amount of force required to fully compress the ball so it can "bounce back" to its original shape for maximum distance. Generally, 80 compression indicates a ball for women and young juniors, 90 compression for men and stronger women and juniors, and 100 compression for better, more powerful players.

Ten years ago, that's all there was, so the lines were clear: two-piece balls for high handicappers, three-piece surlyns for mid-to-low handicappers, and three-piece balatas for tournament players. Today those lines are blurry. Manufacturers have developed "synthetic balatas" that provide the soft feel and high spin rate of natural balata, but are more durable, making them practical buys for more than just the best golfers. Two-piece balls are now available in surlyn or balata, in various compressions, and various dimple patterns that promise better wind control or different trajectories. You even see them on Tour.

To make choices, think of characteristics rather than construction. High handicappers generally want a ball that is durable, flies a long distance, and provides plenty of roll. These will generally be two-piece surlyn balls with high-energy cores made of ultra-hard rubber. They won't provide a lot of feel or backspin, but at that level it's not that important. In fact, a ball with a high spin rate is usually a curse for the high handicapper. If it creates a lot of backspin, it's also more susceptible to the sidespin characteristic of the high handicapper. That means errant shots, hit with a softer, spinning ball, become more errant. The less spin, the straighter they fly.

The basic rule for determining why one ball spins more than another is the ratio of cover to core. A balata ball has a soft, light cover and a hard, heavier core, increasing spin. A two-piece surlyn ball has a harder, heavier cover and a softer, lighter core. With a greater ratio of weight toward the edge of the sphere, spin is reduced.

Distance and durability should still be the top two priorities for middle handicappers, but as they improve they may want a bit more feel and backspin from their ball. Three-piece surlyn balls or two-piece synthetic balata balls are possibilities.

Better players will demand the highest level of feel from their ball. Natural balata is the ultimate "player's" ball, and although developments have been made to make the covers more durable, it doesn't take much to scuff or cut them. They're excellent for tournament play, but perhaps a more practical alternative for day-in, day-out golf is a two- or three-piece ball with a cover made from synthetic balata, which is more resistant to cuts and scuffs. It will provide adequate feel and backspin, yet last longer before becoming unplayable.

Dimple patterns change from manufacturer to manufacturer. Years ago all balls had the same number of dimples, 312. Then, several years ago, manufacturers began changing the dimple patterns on their balls, and the numbers began to change. It was almost as if they were

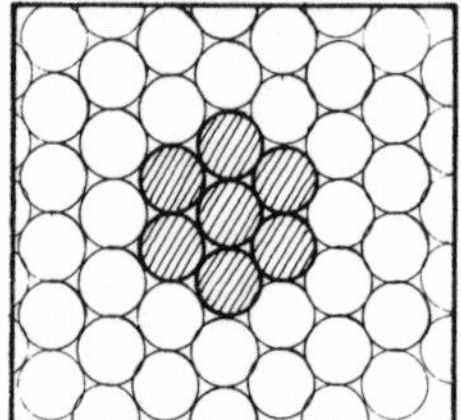
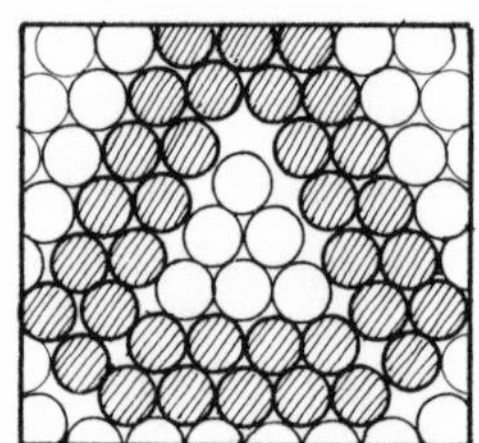
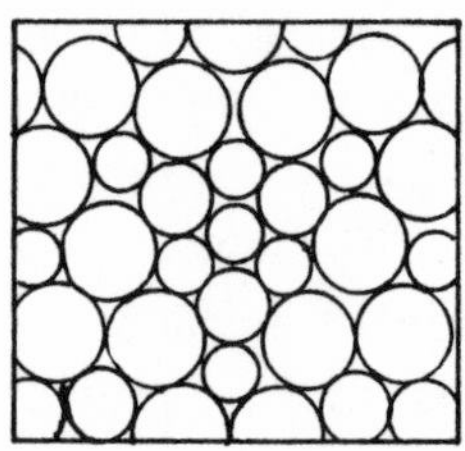

Different dimple patterns

competing to see how many dimples they could put on a golf ball. First, one company produced a ball with 384 dimples. Then another made one with 392. Then 422. Then 492, each time with claims ranging from softer feel to more distance. Today, things have settled a bit. Dimples basically range from 386 to 422, in various patterns: isocahedral, octahedral, dodecahedral, shallow, deep, large, and small.

Dimple size and arrangement affect the trajectory and flight of the ball. Generally, small, deep dimples will produce low trajectory shots, and large, shallow dimples result in higher shots. Compare various balls at the pro shop and you'll see the difference. Keep in mind what trajectory you're looking for. If you play in windy conditions, for example, you'll favor low trajectory balls. Look for a surlyn cover. Here's some possible choices:

- Thirtysomething: two-piece surlyn, high trajectory
  Durable, provides maximum distance
- Bananaballer: two-piece surlyn
  Durable, less backspin means less sidespin
- Bunter: A: three-piece surlyn, low compression
  Durable cover, more feel around green
  B: two-piece surlyn, high trajectory
  Durable, provides maximum distance

- Bomber: A: three-piece surlyn, low trajectory
  Durable cover, more feel, low trajectory for control
  B: synthetic balata two-piece, low trajectory
  Extra feel from thinner cover, better touch
- Player: A: three-piece balata
  Maximum feel and control
  B: synthetic balata two-piece
  More durable, little sacrifice in feel

Bags

Everybody needs a golf bag. You've got to have something to hold those clubs. For all intents and purposes, there are three types of bags: bags made strictly for carrying your clubs as you walk, bags made only for use with a cart, and bags versatile enough to function in both circumstances. Of course, there's no need to "demo" a golf bag or undergo rigorous testing to determine the right bag for you, but you ought to take the time to be practical about buying one.

In this author's perfect world, there would be no motorized carts. Everybody would walk and carry their clubs in lightweight "carry bags" that held their clubs, a few tees and balls, and perhaps a small flask of hot apple cider during the colder months. You couldn't exactly strap them onto the back of a cart, but remember, this is my world: There are no carts.

These carry bags are actually available in this world, and are in fact the least expensive, but as we know, motorized carts are everywhere, and at many courses walking is not permitted. Walk into the bag room of a typical private country club and you'll see that the majority of bags are big, heavy, luggage-like bins made of expensive leather, often with the logo of their favorite equipment manufacturer emblazoned on them. Why? Well, beside being a status symbol—people want to use what pros use—these big "staff" bags are awfully protective of those clubs they hold. Throw the bag on a cart, cinch the strap around it, drive it through a few gopher holes, and the clubs won't feel a thing. They also have so many pockets that they hold just about everything a golfer could possibly need in a span of the four-and-a-half hours it takes to play a round of golf. Dozens of balls, tees, an umbrella, an extra sweater, raingear—throw it all in there. There's room to spare. So, if you never intend to walk a round of golf, consider these big staff bags an option. They're no fun to carry from the baggage claim to the car, and they're the most expensive, but they look good and they do a great job of protecting your clubs.

If, however, you have experienced the joy of walking a golf course in the late afternoon with your clubs on your back, you will try to walk as often as possible. Unfortunately, chances are you'll still have to ride just as often. Your best investment is a bag that can serve double duty: Light enough that it can be carried without breaking your back, and sturdy enough that it can be strapped to a cart and not collapse.

These versatile bags are usually made of nylon, with walls lined with a hard plastic sheeting that protects the clubshafts. Pockets, although not enormous, are plentiful, and store all the needed accessories. Bag manufacturers are working hard to develop bags that combine the trimmings of a staff bag with the convenience of a carryall. A recent trend has been to attach collapsible legs to the bag that open to serve as a stand when the golfer puts the bag down.

Bags usually come with headcovers to protect the heads of your woods. Check and make sure they're included. If not, make the investment. Clubs do a lot of clinking together in the bag. Headcovers will lengthen the life of your clubs, not to mention cutting down on unnecessary noise.

Shoes

How important are golf shoes? Unless you've got a perfectly balanced swing and you play only in the driest weather, you can't play without them. Not only do the spiked soles prevent your feet from sliding around during the swing, but the reinforced uppers protect and support your foot from the stress that comes with the natural motion of the golf swing.

Golf shoes used to be strictly a leather proposition, wing-tipped, saddled, or tassled, leather soled, heavier than street shoes, and not particularly comfortable until they got a some mileage on them. Like any leather shoes, wet weather posed a problem. There were waterproof and water-resistant shoes available, but they were made of vinyl, lacking the good looks and suppleness of leather.

Unless you plan on buying two or three pairs of golf shoes or waiting until the morning dew dries before you tee off, the most practical buy you can make are waterproof shoes. Forget the awkward vinyl uppers. Waterproofing processing has advanced, and today you can find leather shoes that will survive a few raindrops and puddles without shriveling up. With rubber and composite soles and lightweight spikes, much of the cumbersome weight has been removed. Manufacturers have made comfort a priority, so the old standard breaking-in time of a few rounds has lessened considerably.

And if you prefer less of a dress shoe look, athletic shoe manufacturers have joined the party. They bring with them not only a sportier look, but the sensibilities that come with years of making high-performance athletic footwear. Shoes are more versatile and comfortable today than ever before.

By the way, when it comes to things like balls, bags, shoes, and most other golf accessories, our ban on sporting goods stores and golf discount houses is lifted. You don't need a golf course (or a golf pro) to choose a bag or shoes, and you can't demo golf balls anyway. Prices will likely be most expensive at your local pro shop, so go find yourself a bargain.

NINE

Golf Gifts

Golf being such a personal game, how does one go about making a gift of golf equipment? After all, what do your loved ones want more than a new set of clubs for Christmas?

Okay, you can make their dreams come true, but please be careful. If your husband, for example, goes as far as to tell you that he's got his heart set on Brand X's clubs, don't assume that he has any reason to believe that they are the clubs for him other than that he's heard good things about them and likes the way they look.

If you want to buy clubs as a gift, here's the perfect way to do it: Go to your local PGA Professional, and instead of simply buying a set of clubs, work out a clubfitting package with him. Arrange to have two lessons, one for swing and one for clubfitting, to be included with a new set of clubs. He can approximate the cost and give you a gift certificate. Your loved one won't be able to rip the wrapping paper off a shiny new set of clubs, but don't feel bad. This is a bigger, better present.

It's a bit more expensive, too. If you'd like to keep the budget lower, have the gift certificate include the clubs only, with a strong suggestion that he or she not just exchange it for the "dream set," but arrange a proper fitting session with the pro.

On the other hand, clubs aren't the only gift option. Bags, shoes, balls, headcovers, instructional aids, home videos—they're all out there beckoning to the friend or relative of the certifiable golf nut. And there's less risk involved. Who ever heard of "bookfitting" anyway?

Of course, if you really want to save money, give a book . . . maybe one about buying golf equipment the smart way!

TEN

Review

Okay. Just a few more pages and you're free to go find that perfect set of golf clubs. Before you go, though, let's do a quick review to make sure you've got all the bases covered.

First, know the golf club. Know all the components that go into woods, irons, and putters, and what the purpose is of each. You don't want somebody to throw a foreign term at you in the heat of the buying battle.

Know yourself. Being honest about your ability and tendencies is vital if you're going to find clubs that truly help your game.

Know the market. Keep yourself abreast of all the latest equipment news—it's a rapidly changing industry—by reading golf magazines and browsing around golf shops when you have the chance. You'll be a smarter consumer with market knowledge.

Get fitted properly. This is most important. Remember The Five Golden Rules of Buying Clubs:

#1: You can't make an intelligent choice about clubs unless you've hit them first.

#2: Skill level has no correlation to quality of product or fit. All players should have the best equipment possible.

#3: Only a trained teacher of the golf swing can accurately fit a golfer to a set of clubs. Teaching and fitting go hand in hand.

#4: The only lie that counts is the lie at impact, and it can only be measured with an impact board.

#5: Beware of the bulk/clone ploy and other covert maneuvers that aren't aimed at your best interests.

Don't forget the Unofficial Rule of Buying Clubs: *Other than the Golden Rules, there are no rules.* It's perhaps the most important rule of all, because things aren't going to be easy. You're going to run into snags along the way. You won't be able to find the clubs you want, or your pro won't be helpful, or the only golf course is an hour away. Anything could happen. Be persistent, be patient, and try to create the best possible clubfitting experience for yourself. It's not a bad idea to give Henry-Griffets a call (they're based in Hayden Lake, Idaho) and see if any of their professionals are in your area. If not, you're going to have to do your legwork, and push the pro you're dealing with to do the same. It's in your best interests.

At some point, however, you're going to reach the limits of what you can contribute to the clubfitting process, and you're going to have to put your trust in the PGA Professional. If he or she is a quality pro, he'll take care of you. It's in his or her best interests, too: A happy customer is a return customer. Don't be afraid to remind the pro of that.

Above all, once you've found that perfect set of clubs, make all the time and effort you've spent worth it: Get out on the golf course and enjoy yourself.

ELEVEN

Upkeep

If you use this book properly, it can be a real money saver. Make smart choices when you buy clubs and you won't have to shell out another few paychecks a year later because you don't like your new set. But no matter how perfect your clubs are, they are subject to wear and tear. Grips wear out, finishes become dull and chipped, whipping unwinds—regular play means regular upkeep is required, and that costs money.

Ordinarily, you'd give your clubs to your PGA Professional when they need a tune-up. Your pro has been trained in club repair, so you can usually count on a good job. However, like an auto mechanic, your pro will charge you for parts and labor. He or she might charge you $5 a club for regripping, but only half of that $5 represents the costs of the materials. The other half is labor.

Changing grips, as well as some other repairs, is pretty easy. You don't need to be a PGA Professional to do it; you just need the right technique and materials. You'll cut your maintenance costs in half if you learn to do some of your own club repair. The question is, what repairs can you realistically take care of on your own?

Regripping

Here's what you need:

1. Grips
2. Special double-sided tape
3. Grip solvent (paint thinner or gasoline)

4. Sharp X-acto knife (steel shafts only)
5. Heavy-duty syringe (graphite shafts only)
6. Rags

Often your pro will have all the materials you need and will sell them to you at cost. If not, companies like Ralph Maltby's GolfWorks sell equipment and components for golf club assembly and repair. They're a great resource if you're looking to start your own little shop.

1. Start by removing the old grips. If you have steel shafts, you can use an X-acto knife. Place the butt end of the club on a workbench or other solid surface you can cut on, and slice the grip in half from end to end. Then pull the grip off.

If you are regripping graphite-shafted clubs, you can't cut the grips off; you'll damage the shafts with the knife. Instead, use a large syringe filled with grip solvent. Work the needle into the grip at an angle almost parallel to the shaft, until the needle hits the shaft. Inject the solvent into the grip. Using your hands, work the solvent around so the entire inside of the grip is coated. The solvent will loosen the bonds and you can slide the grip off. If you prefer this method of removal, you can use it for steel shafts. It's not quite as fast, but it saves the grip if for some reason you want to reuse it.

2. Clean the old underlisting tape off the shaft by either peeling it or scraping it with a knife (steel shafts only). If it's particularly stubborn, soak a rag in grip solvent and rub vigorously. The tape will loosen. Be sure the shaft is completely clean before applying the new grip tape. Any old bits of tape will form lumps under the new tape, which you'll feel under the grip once you get it on.

3. You have two types of two-sided underlisting tape to choose from: 3/4-inch or two-inch. Don't think that any old double-stick tape will do; grip tape is extremely thin and designed to adhere to rubber when mixed with solvent.

If you're using 3/4-inch tape, start where the bottom of the grip would be, and spiral your way up the shaft until you reach the butt end. Leave an extra two inches hanging off the end so you can cover the hole in the butt end of the shaft. This prevents the solvent from getting inside the shaft and loosening the epoxy that holds the clubhead in place. Allow about 1/8 inch between the windings, avoid any wrinkles, and don't overlap.

Two-inch tape is quicker and easier to use. Simply lay the tape lengthwise along the grip portion of the shaft, and press the sides of the tape around the circumference. Use another small piece of tape to cover the butt end.

If you require thicker grips, use two-inch tape and wrap the shaft as many times as you wish. Each layer of tape represents an extra 1/32 of an inch.

4. For the actual installation, it's helpful to have a vise to hold the club so both hands are free. Using a vise clamp to protect the shaft, secure the club so the toe of the clubhead points straight up and the grip end of the shaft extends over a surface that you don't mind dripping grip solvent on.

Hold the new grip in one hand, and cover the hole in the butt end with your finger. Pour solvent into the open end of the grip with the other hand. Swish it around so the entire inside of the grip gets wet. Pour the solvent out of the grip and over the underlisting tape. Be sure that the butt end of the shaft gets soaked.

Working quickly, pinch the end of the grip open and slide it over the butt end of the shaft. Slide the grip all the way down until it stops.

5. Remove the club from the vise and align the grip so it is square to the clubface. Don't dilly-dally; the solvent dries quickly. Use a rag and solvent to clean any excess tape off the shaft that has been pushed out by the grip. Let the club sit overnight.

The first few clubs you regrip may be tough, but you'll pick it up quickly. With any sort of familiarity with the process, you can regrip an entire set of clubs in 45 minutes or less.

Rewhipping

Nothing may seem less significant than the nylon thread wrapped around the neck of a wood, but whipping thread is a vital component of the construction. Hit a shot on the heel of a wooden club that doesn't have whipping and you'll probably split the neck; hit a few more and the clubhead will break off. Any mis-hit shot puts extreme pressure on the hosel of a club. Stainless steel is unaffected, but because the wood is so thin, it needs reinforcement to withstand the shock of mis-hits. Whipping provides that support.

At the same time, it doesn't take much for the whipping on your woods to start unwinding. The leading edge of an iron can nick the thread, and eventually a nick will lead to a break. Time to get it rewhipped.

Do it yourself. Instead of leaving it overnight with a pro and paying for labor, you can save money and have it ready to go in 15 minutes. All you need is a spool of nylon whipping thread (available through your pro or a components company) and an old cap to a can of shaving cream or of an aerosol can. Again, don't substitute other nylon thread for the real thing. This stuff is thick and is made to absorb shock.

The cap serves as a third hand. Attach it with glue, tape, or nail to the end of your workbench so that you can stick the grip of the club in the open end while you wrap the whipping.

1. With the butt end resting in the cap, tuck the shaft of the club under your right arm so the clubhead points away from you. Don't cut the thread yet; just take the end in your left hand and let the spool sit on the floor so it can unravel freely.

2. Lay about 1/2 inch of the end of the thread lengthwise on the hosel of the club. The tip should point at the clubhead end of the club. With a piece of Scotch, masking, or grip tape, tape the end down so you can start winding where the hosel meets the shaft.

3. Start slowly wrapping the thread over the extended end, making your way down the hosel toward the clubhead. After a few wraps to get started, hold the thread taut with your right hand as you rotate the club with your left. The shaft remains locked under your arm the entire time. Continue turning the club, making sure the thread is taut, until you are four or five turns from the end of the whipping area (you'll see a line from the old whipping).

4. Now it's time to cut the thread. Give yourself a couple of feet to work with. Lay the end of the thread lengthwise over the last loop you've wrapped. Continue wrapping over the thread until you've got one wrap past the whipping line. There should be a big loop of thread sticking out from under the whipping. Slowly and carefully, pull on the end of the whipping. The loop gets smaller. Continue pulling until the loop is gone. Cut off the excess whipping with a craft knife and you're finished. Both ends of the whipping thread should be covered by the wrap, running lengthwise along the back of the neck.

Other Repairs

Lots of other things can be done to keep your clubs in shape. Reshafting, refinishing woods, checking and altering loft and lie, rechroming irons, new inserts, new soleplates—golf clubs are like cars: Spend enough money on them and they'll run like new for years. And yes, you can do all of these repairs yourself, as well. But it requires a serious home workshop, not to mention practice and the luxury of being able to really foul up some perfectly decent clubs in the learning process. Club repair is a great hobby; not too many things are more satisfying than refining a battered old wood and making it look like new. So, if you've got some time on your hands, some money to invest in equipment and supplies, and a taste for craftwork, go for it. Otherwise, let your pro take care of club repair. The most important thing is to make the club playable again. And nobody knows more about that than your pro.

Glossary

Angle of Attack—The degree of descent of the clubhead approaching the ball just before impact.

Backspin—The backward rotation of a golf ball in flight around a horizontal axis.

Backweighting—Weight added to the rear portion of a wood head; designed to move the center of gravity back, promoting a higher trajectory shot.

Blade—The head of an iron club.

Bounce—When the trailing edge of the sole is below the leading edge of the sole in the square hit position.

Bulge—The horizontal curvature on the face of a wood.

Butt End—The larger or grip end of a golf shaft.

Cambered Sole—The curve in the sole of an iron or wood club, from toe-to-heel, leading edge to trailing edge, or both. Also known as Radiused Sole or Rocker Sole.

Classic—Refers to clubs that are from or are throwbacks to the late 1940s to mid-1960s. Generally made of persimmon wood, forged irons, and flanged or blade putters.

Clubface—The outlined or defined hitting surface of a wood or iron.

Counterbalancing—Reducing the club's swingweight by adding weight to the grip end. Total weight increases and swingweight decreases.

Crown—The highest point of the top of a wood head.

Cycolac—An injection-molded plastic used for face inserts in wood clubs.

Deep Face—Refers to a wood head that has a higher than normal face height.

Face Progression—Measurement of the distance from the centerline of the shaft or hosel to the front leading portion of the clubface in both woods and irons.

Fiber—Insert material used in the faces of persimmon wood heads. Made of compressed, vulcanized paper, it is softer than most insert materials and appeals to the better player.

Firing Pin—A circular piece of metal, usually aluminum or brass, installed in the center of some types of inserts.

Flange—Refers to the elongation of the trailing edge of an iron or putter.

Foreweighting—Depositing weight in the face area of a club, done to bring the center of gravity forward in the clubhead. Promotes a lower shot trajectory.

Forging—One of the processes for forming iron heads. A metal bar is hammered under pressure into the rough shape of an iron head, then cooled, ground, and polished into final shape.

Frequency Matching—Method of measuring consistency of shaft flex throughout a set of clubs.

Gooseneck—See Offset Hosel.

Graphite—A pure carbon mineral made into fibers, mixed with a resin, and formed into a golf shaft. Characteristically lightweight and strong.

Grip—The portion of the club designed for the hands to hold. Usually made of rubber, and occasionally, leather.

Head Width—The distance from the farthest forward point of the leading edge to the farthest rear point of the back line.

Heel—The portion of the clubface closest to the hosel.

Heel-Toe Weighting—Distribution of weight in which weight is taken from the center of a wood, iron, or putter, and relocated equally to the toe and heel. Designed to improve off-center hits by adding weight away from the sweet spot.

Hosel—Or neck, the portion of the clubhead that holds the shaft.

Impact Board—Large board designed to fit a golfer to clubs with the correct lie. Balls are hit off the board; impact leaves a mark on the sole of the club, indicating how far from center the lie is.

Insert—A piece of material placed into the face of a wood head, designed to improve the durability of the face from impact between the ball and the clubhead. Usually made of Cycolac, epoxy, fiber, aluminum, or graphite.

Investment Casting—A method of producing iron heads and metal woods. A mold is made, and a wax is cast from the mold. The wax is dipped into a ceramic mixture, which hardens into a shell. The shell is heated, the wax melts away, and molten steel is poured into the shell. It cools and produces a clubhead.

Kevlar—High-impact plastic used in bullet-proof vests. Also used occasionally for clubheads, and mixed with graphite to make shafts.

Kick Point—Point of greatest flex on a shaft. High kick point means near the hands; low kick point indicates greatest flex near the hosel.

Laminated—A type of wood head made by gluing thin strips of maple together.

Lead Tape—adhesive tape backed with a thin layer of lead. Used to add weight to clubheads.

Length (club)—The distance from the heel portion of the sole to the top of the grip.

Lie—The angle formed by the centerline of the shaft and the ground when the clubhead is properly soled, with the clubface square to the target.

Loft—The angle formed by the centerline of the clubface and the centerline of the shaft. The property that produces airborne shots.

Low Profile—Iron heads whose face heights are lower than the average.

Offset Hosel—A hosel whose centerline is set ahead of the leading edge of the clubface.

Perimeter Weighting—Process of weighting a club whereby most of the weight is placed in the toe, heel, and sole of the clubhead, rather than the center.

Persimmon—A type of hardwood tree, from the ebony family, from which some wood heads are made. The tree is native to parts of North America and the Far East.

Roll—The vertical curvature built from crown to sole on the face of a wood head.

Scoring—The lines cut, stamped, or cast into the face of a wood or iron head.

Set Makeup—The combination of golf clubs in any set. United States Golf Association rules state that no golfer may play with more than 14 clubs at a time.

Shaft Flex—The measurement of a shaft's resistance to bending under a given stress.

Shallow Face—Wood heads that have a face height less than standard.

Sole—The bottom of a wood or iron head that would normally touch the ground.

Soleplate—A metal plate attached to the bottom of wood heads to prevent wear to the wood. Also used to increase the weight of the clubhead. Usually made of aluminum, steel, or brass.

Sole Weighting—Distributing the weight on a wood or iron head as low in the head as it can be placed. Promotes a higher trajectory shot.

Strong Loft—Less loft than standard for any given club. Generally produces more distance.

Swingweight—A measurement that indicates the distribution of weight in a golf club from grip to clubhead. It is expressed in a letter/number combination (C-4, C-8, D-0, D-2, etc.).

Tipped Shaft—A shaft in which a small portion of the tip, or clubhead end of the shaft, is cut off. Practiced by better players, tipping produces a stiffer feel.

Toe—The furthest point outward on a wood or iron head.

Top Line—The top of an iron head where the face and back meet.

Torque—The amount of rotational twist that occurs in a golf shaft during the swing. Prevalent mostly in graphite shafts.

Trajectory—The pattern or shape of the flight of a golf ball with respect to its height and direction.

Upright—When the lie angle is more erect or vertical than standard.

Utility Wood—A wood designed for play from the rough and bad lies. Often a higher-lofted clubhead (5–7-wood loft) is combined with a longer than standard shaft. Occasionally features rails or ridges on the sole to aid digging action from bad lies.

Weak Loft—More loft than standard for any given club. Generally produces less distance.

Whipping—The string wrapping that covers the neck of a wood club. Prevents the wooden hosel from cracking from the jar of repeated impact.

INDEX